Bond with Your Heart; Train with Your Brain

Techniques for Training & Motivating Humans & Other Animals

JOEL SILVERMAN

Host of Animal Planet's "GOOD DOG U" and
the syndicated TV Series "DOG & CAT TRAINING WITH JOEL SILVERMAN"

Doce Blant Publishing

BOND WITH YOUR HEART; TRAIN WITH YOUR BRAIN
by JOEL SILVERMAN

Copyright ©2013 Joel Silverman
All rights reserved.

This book or part thereof may not be reproduced in any form by any means, electronic or mechanical, including photocopy, recording, or otherwise, or by any information storage and retrieval system, except as may be expressly permitted in writing from the publisher as provided by the United States of America copyright law. Requests for permission should be addressed to Doce Blant Publishing, Attn: Rights and Permissions Dept., 32565-B Golden Lantern St. #323, Dana Point, CA 92629

Published by
Doce Blant Publishing, Dana Point, CA 92629
www.doceblantpublishing.com

Cover by Fiona Jayde Media
Edited by Ren Cummins

ISBN: 978-1-7320807-1-3

Printed in the United States of America
www.doceblant.com

This book is dedicated to my best friend DUKE,
the gentle giant whose commercials entertained millions, and
who put a smile on the face of everyone he met.

Everyone has had a best friend. Mine had four legs.

TABLE OF CONTENTS

Introduction	vii
CHAPTER 1 **RELATIONSHIPS AND TRUST**	1
CHAPTER 2 **OPERANT CONDITIONING**	13
CHAPTER 3 **REWARDS**	19
CHAPTER 4 **CORRECTIONS**	35
CHAPTER 5 **MARINE MAMMAL BEHAVIOR**	53
CHAPTER 6 **PREDICTABLITY**	73
CHAPTER 7 **BODY LANGUAGE**	89
CHAPTER 8 **MOTIVATION**	97
CHAPTER 9 **PRACTICE MAKES PERFECT**	105
A Few Last Cues	113
About Joel Silverman	114
Certification Courses	115

INTRODUCTION

You may be scratching your head and asking yourself why you just purchased a book by an animal trainer about how to enhance your skills in training and management.

For much of my life, I've made a living training animals for movies, TV shows, and commercials. Early in my career, I worked with a wide variety of marine mammals in theme parks. Over 10 years ago, I had the distinct pleasure of hosting my first TV series on what was then the new Animal Planet television channel: "GOOD DOG U." And for the past 20 years, I've sold thousands of dog training videos.

What I've learned in those 30 years is this: What goes on in the minds of most animals is much like what we experience in ours. Why? Because humans are animals.

I'm not an "animal behaviorist" who's a professor at some university and whose name is followed by a series of capital letters, but I have over 30 years of hands-on experience in working with our furry and not-so-furry friends. I've learned, too, through that experience, that much of what works in building relationships with dogs, cats and marine mammals works with human "animals" as well.

Notice I said *relationships*, and not training. To teach most animals effectively, especially the more "intelligent" ones, you need first to develop a relationship with them—a relationship based on trust.

What I hope you will take away from this book are some of the principles of animal behavior and how to apply many of the same animal behavioral training techniques that I've learned over my career to your situation, whether you're looking for ways to build a better relationship with your children, managing one person or a small staff, or teaching people of all ages, but especially kids.

You'll learn that much of my experience comes from the training of dogs, dolphins, sea lions, killer whales, and a variety of other animals. Like people, these are all very intelligent animals with an incredible potential for learning.

In order for us to learn efficiently, we both need many of the same things, including:

- *Direction – We need to have a game plan and small goals.*
- *Good communication – Everything needs to be presented in a simple and easy manner.*
- *Guidance – We need to know our leaders/teachers/ coaches are there for us, and that we can trust them.*
- *Individualistic learning – Because of the variety in people and animals, we all learn at different speeds. What may work for one may not be effective for another.*
- *Motivation – We both need the drive to work and a desire to complete goals.*
- *Rewards – We need something to give us a reason to complete a job or achieve the goal.*
- *Corrections - We need to be shown when we do things incorrectly in ways that do not jeopardize the relationship that's been established.*

Getting the best out of your children, staff, or students is really all about building relationships, establishing and maintaining good communication, and letting the people you parent, supervise, or teach what is and what is not expected of them.

In some chapters, I will go into specific detail about how we train certain animal behaviors. In others, I'll spend more time talking about how those training techniques can be modified to work with humans.

In any case, this book is likely different from any other you've come across. First, it will educate you about how some of your favorite animals are trained. Most importantly, though, I hope it will help you begin to imagine the world as seen through the eyes of the most intelligent and amazing animals in the world...your children, employees and students.

Bond with your heart; train with your brain

CHAPTER 1

RELATIONSHIPS AND TRUST

The one thing that separates a good animal trainer from a great animal trainer is that the great animal trainer has found a way to build an awesome relationship with the animal he's training. As I look at back at my career and recall some of the best animal trainers I've had the opportunity to work with, it's obvious that they were the ones who were creative, established a trusting relationship with their students, and, above all, made the learning fun. Make no mistake—some good animal trainers have accomplished a great deal with some of the animals they've trained without building a relationship, but I find myself asking, "How much *more* would they have gotten out of their animals if they'd bonded with them and established lasting relationships?"

The best animal trainers have also been the best communicators. The main reason each was so successful was that he always put himself, as best he could, *in the place of the animal he was working with*. This means that, as he was training the animal, when that animal did something correctly, he always gave it the most reinforcing things—the things that the animal wanted most—at the most appropriate time.

Animal training is really all about chemistry. If you've watched my TV series or seen any of my videos, you know that I always stress that no two trainers are identical, and no two animals are exactly the same, either. It's the bonding, the chemistry between an animal and its trainer that makes each relationship so special and unique.

Build the Relationship First

Let's start with the animal most of us have some experience with—dogs.

The most important idea in training a dog is to understand that a dog is the one animal that seems innately to want to please you. He/she *wants* to be your "best friend."

I have found that many new dog owners don't understand that establishing a relationship with a dog actually lays the foundation for training it. The animal works for *you*, the trainer—and not to get a treat or other reward. Think about your favorite teacher in school—were you really working for the grade?

Let's say you decide to rescue a dog from the animal shelter, and you bring the dog home. You now have a choice as to how to deal with this new addition to your home. You can do what many people do, namely try to begin to train your dog within the next few days.

If you've read my book *What Color is Your Dog?* you probably know that just like people, dogs have many different types of personalities. Straight from the shelter, chances are that a dog will either be a little shy or a little aggressive.

If the dog is a little shy and you begin to train him, he'll probably make a few mistakes along the way, as any dog will. Once he makes those mistakes, you'll probably want to correct him. But when you've had a shy dog for such a short period of time and you attempt to correct him (sometimes even when the correction is nothing more than saying "no"), there is a good chance that the correction will scare him and make him a lot *more* shy.

If a dog leans toward being aggressive and you begin to train him, as with the shy dog, he too will probably make a few mistakes along the way. And, once he makes those mistakes, you'll want to correct him as well; but when you've had an aggressive dog for such a short period of time and you correct him, there's a good chance he will become even more aggressive towards you, unlike the shy dog.

In both of these scenarios, whether your new dog is shy or aggressive, he is likely just "protecting" himself. Why? *The dog doesn't know you yet.*

The reason the training seems ineffective is that it *isn't* a training issue. It's a *trust* issue. A trusting relationship between the dog and its new owner was not given time to develop.

Okay, let's consider those same two types of dogs again. Let's say that you decide to rescue a dog from the animal shelter, and you bring the dog home. This time, you take that shy dog and do nothing more than take a few weeks to build a trusting relationship with the animal. NO attempts at training take place during this time. The only thing you seek to accomplish during this period is to find all the things the animals likes, and discover all the things the animal *dislikes*.

As you begin to spend time with the shy dog, you're going to find that the dog is afraid of certain things. Those are the things you're going try to *eliminate happening* for the time being. At the same time, there are some things you're going to find that the dog *does* like, such as certain treats, and those are the things *you are going want to introduce*. If you begin to eliminate all the things the dog *doesn't* like, and increase the things that the dog *does* like when you're around him, the dog will "figure out" on his own that he has every reason to want to be around you. Most importantly, you have now begun to build a *trusting relationship.* He trusts that you're going to put him in situations that don't scare him, and he begins to "look forward" to the great things that you're going to share with him.

The same approach works with an aggressive dog. This time you take that aggressive dog and *do nothing more* than take a few weeks to build a trusting relationship with the animal. Again, no training is done during that time. The only things that are accomplished during those first few weeks are finding the things the animal likes and discovering the things that the animal is afraid of.

As you begin to spend time with this more aggressive dog, you're going to find that the dog acts more aggressively toward certain things (or perhaps certain *people*). You're going to try to eliminate those things and/or avoid those people initially.

At the same time, you're going to find what the dog likes, such as certain treats. As with the shy dog, those are the only things you will introduce in the beginning.

Then, just as with the shy dog, once you begin to eliminate all the things that cause the dog to be aggressive and introduce the things the dog likes when you're around him, he will have every reason to want to be around you; then, since he's no longer afraid, he will become less aggressive.

People

How does this apply to people? Well, you can be the teacher of 20 smart students, but if they have no desire to be in the class with you or if they haven't developed respect for and trust in you, they will never likely learn at their highest potential.

You can be a manager or a supervisor with the best employees working for you, but if you haven't spent the time to develop a trusting relationship, if they aren't comfortable with you in the workplace, even the naturally hardest-working employees will never likely work up to their true potential.

You can be a parent who has great discipline, and good communication with your child. Your child may even do exceptionally well in school; but if the trust between you and your child has not been built and she doesn't feel safe with you...You get the picture.

I can't say it enough: the most important key to developing a good relationship is trust.

I truly believe that coaches, management trainers and teachers quite often jump into training and teaching before they've established trust with those they work with. Expectations for performance too often take precedence over development of a sense of trust and safety. Parents' expectations can start out a little too high as well. (We've all seen situations where it seems like a parent wants something for their kids when the kids don't really care.)

The point is that when someone whose job is to teach, coach or train makes the environment fun, enjoyable and safe, animals and people are motivated to be there, and training sessions go much more efficiently.

Getting Started

The best animal trainers I've met and worked with over the years are naturally kind and generous people. I don't think it is an accident that some of the best *people* trainers I've met in my lifetime were also very nice people too, including my parents, who were both excellent and well-regarded teachers.

I'm convinced that the reason my parents were as successful as they were is that they practiced *empathy*, and that the most effective leaders and animal trainers put themselves in the "shoes" of the animals and people they work with. They strive to give both rewards and corrections at the right moments, when they are most likely to produce the best results without negatively impacting the good relationships they have.

Think of your best friend or significant other. Why did you want to meet and spend time with her? What qualities and traits caused you to want to be around him? It is unlikely that you became best friends in an hour, a day, or even a week. It took time.

But, as you started spending more time together and got to know each other, you began to share things you might not have shared with other people. You took the time to create a special bond based on trust—and that's the trust that I'm talking about.

Putting Yourself in an Animal's "Shoes"

A good animal trainer will always take the time to get to know an animal and motivate it to want to be around him. Once he identifies some things the animal likes, he will give it those things as rewards at the most opportune time. And, when the animal does something *incorrectly*, he will give it the correction *that animal* needs to get the message across, doing it as gently as possible in order not to jeopardize the animal's trust in him.

Likewise, the best teachers I know take the time to develop relationships with the people they work with, getting to know each student personally and individually. They understand, too, that *each person is different*, and they take the time to develop a unique and special relationship on that basis. If someone takes the time to get to know and understand us, we believe we're important to them, and if we know we are important to someone, we want to do our best for them.

Take a Look at Yourself First

If you're a teacher, take a look at your students. How are you perceived by them?

- *How do they look at you as their teacher?*
- *Do they see you as a leader, in charge?*
- *Are you someone they can trust?*
- *Do they feel important?*
- *Do they each feel comfortable enough to ask questions?*
- *Do they know what you expect of them?*

With whatever age students you're teaching, the same thing applies—if you feel that you are not liked, listened to or trusted, the first thing you need to do is take a good look at yourself. As a teacher, you want students to feel comfortable enough to ask you questions any time they need to. When they don't have that comfort, they may lose valuable chances to learn. You can't answer questions that aren't asked.

If you manage a group of people, ask yourself these questions:
- *How am I perceived by the people I supervise?*
- *Are they intimidated by me?*
- *Do they seem to like me?*
- *Do they listen to me?*
- *Do they work up to their best potential?*
- *Am I someone they can trust?*

If you feel that you are not liked, listened to, trusted, or perceived in a positive way by the people you manage, the first thing you need to do is take an honest look at yourself. There may be something you have done, or perhaps *not* done, that has given the people you manage a negative perception of you.

If you're a parent, think of your kids. How are you perceived by them?

- *How do they look at you as their parent?*
- *Do they feel confident in your leadership?*
- *Are you someone they trust to go to with their feelings?*
- *Do they feel important to you? Needed by you?*
- *Do they ask you questions?*

The cold hard truth is this: if you aren't providing an emotionally safe and trusting environment for your children, the first thing you need to do is take a look at yourself. In being a parent, it is important that your children tell you things that are bothering them and ask you questions any time they need to. If they don't feel that they can talk to you or don't seem to want to be around you, they lose valuable chances to learn from you and grow. Now, isn't that what being a parent is really about?

I've seen numerous training problems stem from the fact that a dog only wanted to be around his trainer in certain situations. I've also seen instances where the only time an animal exhibited "negative" behavior was when the owner was trying to train him.

Was it merely coincidence? I don't think so; rather, I think the problems developed because the "experience of being trained" had become a negative one.

For the same exact reason, employees and students often fail to work to their full potentials—the learning or working environment is experienced as negative. Whether we're talking about people or animals, the training environment is key.

Can a Bad Situation Be Changed?

Yes, fortunately, it can. Here's an example based on the situation I mentioned above, when a dog developed a negative attitude with respect to training sessions.

I suggested to the owners that they go back almost to the beginning, and focus on developing trust. Here were my recommendations:

- *Find as many things as possible that the dog clearly likes.*
- *Introduce those things to the dog a few times a day at certain times.*

What these particular owners discovered is that finding out what the dog liked wasn't hard, because they already knew the answer. They had had the dog long enough to have noticed what he got excited about—in this case, a few different types of treats.

I stressed to them that no matter how much the dog seemed to *want* to be trained, *under no circumstances were they to attempt to train the dog.* All I asked them to do was to simply give the dog a couple of the treats four or five times a day.

Implementing this simple technique resulted in two things. First, they began to recognize what the dog liked. The other thing it involved was becoming unpredictable, a concept I will go into more depth in later on. Using the concept, the owners were "unpredictable" with respect to *when* they gave their dog the treats they knew he liked. The dog never knew when he was going to get a treat or how much of it he was going to get. In the end, he began to associate the treats with his *owners* and not with particular behaviors.

Within a few days, the dog was following them around the house, waiting to see if they had the treats, but here's where the picture began to change. In the next few weeks, the dog started to follow them around the house *even when they didn't have the things the dog liked.*

As time went on, they began to retrain the dog using the dog's developed interest and desire to be around them as the primary reward. They began to incorporate those things into the training sessions too, and the dog began to associate "good things" with the training sessions. The dog's attitude totally changed!

If early on in a school year your relationship with a student doesn't start off right, don't worry. There's still time to correct course. Take the time now to go back and build or strengthen your relationship. As you look at the people you train and supervise on the job, make establishing a better relationship your first priority. With respect to your children, shore up their comfort and trust in you.

In any training endeavor, build a trusting relationship first. It becomes the foundation that will help you get the best out of your kids, students or employees.

CHAPTER 2

OPERANT CONDITIONING

Now that you've begun to develop a trusting relationship, let's begin to talk about training, starting with a basic technique known as *operant conditioning*.

The definition of operant conditioning is "a method of learning in the animal field that occurs through rewards and punishments for behavior." It is also defined as "the use of consequences to modify the occurrence and form of behavior."

Through operant conditioning, over time, animals (and people) make associations between certain behaviors and consequences of that behavior. Some consequences are natural, some imposed. In this case, the consequence for a behavior is dictated by the trainer. (This is an idea that a psychologist named B.F. Skinner developed many years ago.)

There are four possible consequences for behavior in operant conditioning:

Positive Reinforcement: You give your dog a cue to sit, he sits, and you reward him. This will increase the likelihood that the behavior will occur again. (EASY ENOUGH, RIGHT?)

Negative Reinforcement: This occurs when a behavior (response) is followed by the *removal* of an *aversive* stimulus (commonly seen as unpleasant), thereby *increasing* the behavior's frequency. You give your dog the cue to sit, he does not, so you apply upward pressure on the leash; this gets your dog to sit. This serves to increase the likelihood that the dog will sit when you say "sit" in the future in order *to avoid the pressure on its throat*. However, it can be (and often is) argued that this is actually a type of punishment. Many behaviorists argue that because this is not pleasant, that what the dog actually learns is how to avoid being "choked." (OW!! NOT FUN FOR THE POOCH!!)

Positive Punishment: Also called "punishment by contingent stimulation" occurs when a behavior (response) is *followed* by an aversive consequence, such as introducing a shock or loud noise, resulting in a decrease in that behavior. Here's an example of positive punishment. You give your dog the cue to sit, he lies down instead, and you jerk him onto his feet with the leash. This involves the presentation of a bad consequence (jerking the leash) when a certain response is performed. It's "positive," not because the consequence is perceived as good, but because *it doesn't involve taking something away*, and increases the likelihood that the dog will not lie down when you tell him to sit. (OUCH!!)

Negative Punishment: Also called "punishment by contingent *withdrawal*" occurs when a behavior (response) is followed by the *removal* of a *favorable* stimulus, such as taking away a child's toy following an undesired behavior. Another example would be telling a dog to "sit," and if the dog lies down, *you* eat the treat you were about to give the dog. This decreases the likelihood of frequency of the dog repeating the undesired behavior. (NOW, THAT'S CONFUSING!)

Let's review the differences between "reinforcement" and "punishment."

- **Reinforcement** is *"an event, a circumstance, or a condition that increases the likelihood that a given response will recur."*
- **Punishment** is the *"presentation of an adverse event or outcome that causes a decrease in the behavior it follows."*

Behaviorists add that there are two kinds of punishment:

- **Positive** *punishment involves the presentation of an unfavorable event or outcome in order to weaken the response it follows.*
- **Negative** *punishment occurs when a favorable event or outcome is removed after a behavior occurs.*

In many cases, especially those involving marine mammal training, what is referred to as punishment may be referred to as a *correction*, which in most cases may be nothing more than asking the animal to repeat the behavior again, repeating it until he gets it right, or ignoring the animal for a few seconds. In dog training, it might be gently moving the animal into a certain position.

If you look up the word "punishment" in the dictionary, you will find one definition that describes it as "suffering, pain, severe, rough, or disastrous treatment." That's not what I'm talking about here. If you punish a dog who responds to something incorrectly in this way, you can injure the animal and seriously ruin the trust that you have so carefully built. With the wrong type of training technique, one which truly punishes animals, I've seen animal relationships destroyed in weeks, days, and even minutes. I consider any action that results in severe or disastrous treatment as incredibly inhumane.

I now use the word "correction" rather than punishment. Be assured that at no time do I use harsh techniques of any kind with the animals I train.

Corrections

A correction can be a variety of different trainer responses based upon the individual animal. The "message" sent to the animal when a correction is used is simply that *the behavior displayed is not acceptable.* Understanding the intent of correction and applying it in the right way will result in successful communication to an animal that his behavior wasn't correct, without scaring it or jeopardizing the animal's trust in you.

When it comes to training any animal, he will be wrong at times, and sometimes he'll be wrong *a lot*. That's OK. Any animal, including the human animal, may never learn to do something *right* unless he first does something *wrong*. It isn't difficult to see that if you are too harsh with someone when correcting, especially early on, you can undermine the trusting relationship you've worked so hard to build with him or her.

This should be a major consideration whether you're interacting with your children, managing a group of employees, or are trying to establish a relationship with a student. Quite often, a correction to an employee or student might be nothing more than gentle ways of letting one know that he or she did something incorrectly.

However, in much the same way as with an animal, when a correction is made in a detrimental way, the trust and relationship can be destroyed very quickly.

In later chapters, we'll go into more detail about how to correct without affecting an animal's attitude and motivation.

But first let's talk about rewards.

CHAPTER 3
REWARDS

One of the things that drew me into the marine mammal and dog training fields was the fact that the training styles at the time were based primarily on *positive reinforcement.* Simply put, this means that the animal is rewarded by the trainer for doing something correctly. In my opinion, though, it goes so much deeper than that because it really involves the animal's *understanding,* connecting that he did something correctly with the reward that follows.

Even as a kid, I remember seeing a dog doing something correctly, followed by its trainer[1] almost always following the behavior with a treat. I still see that type of training taking place, though more advanced trainers have taken their methods to a whole different level. The point they want to get across to the animal is that he *did the behavior correctly.* Notice I mean *communicating* to the animal that he did the behavior correctly, not necessarily *rewarding* the animal. Communicating to the animal is something that should happen *before* rewarding the animal.

So how is this communication achieved? It depends upon the species of animal and the particular animal that the trainer is training. Quite often it might be nothing more than a sound or other affirmation. That sound would generally be followed by a variety of things the animal likes—it might be a reward or another behavior, but it might also be followed with absolutely nothing.

---

[1] In this book, I will use the word trainer inclusively to refer to animal owners, professional trainers and teachers/coaches.

This sound or affirmation (e.g., petting) is what, in the profession, is also called a "bridge," defined as what happens in the time between when an animal performs a desired behavior and when he receives a reward. As you will see later when I talk about training marine mammals, the use of a "bridge" plays a huge role in training. Because these types of animals live and perform in the water, a certain amount of time often passes between the performance of the behavior and its reward.

Change

For most new trainers, an important thing to know is that CHANGE IS REINFORCING to most intelligent animals. What this means is that when a trainer begins to add variety, changing things up, that alone can be a rewarding experience for the animal. Creative trainers who offer the most variation in their training routines are often the most successful ones.

What are some of the things the trainer can vary when rewarding an animal? Give it the reward that most reinforces its behavior at that particular time.

For example, if we're talking about a golden retriever:

- *The dog may like different types of dog treats made from crunchy dog biscuits.*
- *He may like different types of treats that are chewy.*
- *He may like treats made from real cheese, turkey, or beef.*
- *He may like to chase a variety of balls.*
- *He might like to tug on a variety of rags and toys*

Mixing the rewards and adding a lot of variety makes things more interesting and fun for the animal.

Marine Mammals

Because they are different from animals trained on land, marine mammal trainers have different ways of communicating to them that a behavior was performed correctly. For example, during a show in a theme park, if the animal is a sea lion, walrus, or otter, you're likely to see the trainers using a clicker or blowing a high pitched whistle. The sound of the clicker or whistle lets the animal know that he did the behavior correctly.

However, if you watch very closely, you will notice that trainers don't always follow the sound of the clicker with food. They may click the clicker and move on to another behavior, cue the animal to perform up to 10 separate behaviors before he is actually rewarded, or they may click the clicker and just pet the animal.

If you're watching the trainer working with dolphins or killer whales, you won't hear a clicker. Instead you'll hear a *whistle*. The sound of the whistle will mean the exact same thing to the dolphin or whale that the clicker means to the sea lion—it is an affirmation. And just as with a sea lion, you might see the dolphin or whale perform more than one behavior before the trainer actually rewards him.

Just as with the golden retriever described earlier, it is essential, while training, that the trainer *not* become predictable—that he varies both the reward and the timing of it.

What do you think would happen if the trainer were to consistently give a reward to the animal every time he clicked the clicker? In other words, what if, after every "bridge," he rewarded the animal?

Think about it from the animal's point of view: If the trainer were to reward the animal consistently, the animal would begin to anticipate the reward *every time he hears the click*. As time went on, the association of click and reward would become stronger—the trainer would now have become *predictable*. It is, therefore, essential that the trainer add variation; most importantly, he's got to change things up on a regular basis once the behavior is learned.

The "message" marine mammal trainers want to send to the animals they're working with is this: If you do a behavior correctly, you may get one fish, a few fish, a bucket of fish, or no fish at all. This method creates an environment of *un*predictability.

Varied Reinforcement Schedule (VRS)

Some of the best marine mammal trainers use what is called a "Varied Reinforcement Schedule" or VRS. This philosophy is based on the principle that change is reinforcing, which B.F. Skinner demonstrated. (He's that guy in the picture at the beginning of Chapter 2.)

What Skinner did was put a rat in a cage. Inside the cage was a small lever which, when depressed, would release a pellet of food. One day, out of curiosity (and a little coincidence), the rat pressed the lever.

As soon as the rat pressed the lever, a tiny piece of food fell right to where the rat was positioned. After eating the food, the rat pressed the lever again, and once again, a piece of food appeared. Soon, the rat began to press the lever over and over—it had "learned" it would be rewarded with food every time he hit the lever, and actually increased the frequency and speed with which he pressed it. What happened, of course, is that the rat became *conditioned* to associate pressing the lever with the appearance of the food reward.

Then, Skinner thought, what if one day, all of a sudden, the rat hit the lever and a piece of food *didn't* fall? What would happen then?

Remember that based on what he had learned, the rat had come to "understand" that he would always be rewarded for hitting the lever. If your answer was that the rat would press it again, you would be right.

But what do you think happened when he pressed it again and *still* no food appeared? Well, there was some increased agitation, but instead of giving up, the rat actually began to press the lever with even more pressure and frequency—his attitude and drive increased!

A varied reinforcement schedule, as the name suggests, involves the trainer rewarding the animal in an inconsistent, or variable, manner. The greatest thing about a varied reinforcement schedule is that once an animal is conditioned to perform a behavior, he no longer anticipates a particular reward at a particular time because the reinforcement happens on a seemingly random basis.

VRS is a method used extensively in the training of both marine mammals and dogs. I prefer to use this method for a number of reasons, but mostly because it makes me far less predictable. By changing things up so the animal knows neither what type of reinforcement is coming nor how often it's going to come, it keeps the animal "guessing." The training session provides for a much more reinforcing environment for the animal because the trainer now has a wide variety of things he can offer the animal to make the learning experience interesting.

When you combine varied reinforcement with the understanding that all animals are different, creativity comes into play. Once you better understand the animal you're training and what rewards reinforce the behaviors you want him to exhibit, you can start changing things up, making the training session even more fun for the animal. After all, he's with you, one of his favorite people! And that's the most reinforcing thing of all.

As an aside, while it is a fact that animals like change, and while change is reinforcing, when an animal exhibits an *incorrect or undesirable* behavior, VRS plays no role. When an animal does something incorrectly, it is crucial that the trainer not use VRS. Instead, the trainer should focus on using the *exact same correction* EVERY time. Because change itself is experienced as a reward by some animals, you can unintentionally reinforce the very behavior you want to eliminate.

In summary, animals respond well to variable rewards, both in terms of 1) the reward itself and 2) when the reward is and isn't given. This change doesn't need to happen all the time, but what is important is that it does. It's up to us, the trainers, to dictate *when* that change occurs.

With dog training, much like with marine mammal training, effective training primarily involves positive reinforcement—when the dog does something right, the trainer rewards him with something he likes. The great thing about working with dogs is that they enjoy a variety of things, and each of those things can be used as a reward.

Many dogs will work for a trainer simply because of the relationship that has been established. In most situations, however, the greater the number and variety of rewards the trainer is able to offer the animal, the more likely the results will be positive.

If you are training either a Labrador or golden retriever, for example, both of which have incredible "prey drives," you will find that they will not only work for a food treat, but for a toy as well. There may even be a variety of both toys and treats that dog will work for, so once the trainer finds the thing or things that are reinforcing to the dog, he can use them to reward the dog when training a particular behavior, and use them until the behavior is fully trained.

Here's where the training approach takes a turn. *Once the desired behavior is learned, the strategy changes.*

Carrying around pet treats can become a bit of a hassle so weaning the dog away from expecting a treat or toy reward is in order. To do this, the trainer will begin giving a tactile reward (e.g., petting the dog) along with the treat. This way, the animal receives two rewards at the same time. Once the animal is used to that, the trainer will begin to fade out the food reward. SLOWLY.

The process might start by the trainer's giving both rewards together, consistently, for about a week. Then, the trainer will reduce the number of times he gives a food reward with the tactile reward—maybe giving food with petting 75% of the time and only the tactile reward the other 25% of the time. After a week, he will begin to fade out the food reward even more to where he is giving the animal the food with a tactile reward together only 50% of the time. After another week, he will provide both food and tactile awards only 25% of the time, and then go down one more step—giving a food reward only 10% of the time while never removing the tactile reward. He has now conditioned the animal to respond to and enjoy a tactile reward alone. Getting the desired behavior from the dog no longer depends on a food reward.

Rewards and People

Hopefully you've begun to see the science of how rewarding works with some of our most intelligent animals, especially the fact that over time, rewards don't have to be given every time an animal does something correctly. However, whether the animal is a pet or a marine mammal in a theme park show, it's important that trainers not lose sight of the primary goal—communicating that the animal did what you wanted him to.

People need the same thing—ongoing feedback when we have met expectations and rewards for meeting agreed-upon goals. But because the human animal is so much more advanced than even the most intelligent of dogs and marine mammals, parents, teachers and managers can be even more creative in selecting appropriate rewards.

The biggest difference between the animals we train and people is that because of our higher intelligence, we learn much more quickly than with animals. As children grow older and language develops, the rewards become less tangible and more internal. Even so, the philosophy of a varied reinforcement schedule can provide parents, teachers and managers with a framework for keeping the home, class and workplace interesting and fun. With people, affirmation from trusted leaders is especially important. I can speak from experience.

For eight weeks at the end of 2005, I had the unique opportunity to work in southern France training a dog for the movie "A Good Year." While it was a great paying job, and I enjoyed working with the movie's leading actor, Russell Crowe, the greatest reward came from the director, Ridley Scott. After the movie was completed, Ridley took the time to tell me how much he appreciated my work.

That affirmation from one of the top directors in the entertainment industry meant the world to me. Having someone I respected as much as I did Ridley tell me that I did a good job meant a great deal to me at the time, almost as much as the money. The point is that it's really that simple—people need affirmation from those around them, feedback that they did something well and are appreciated for it.

But...there *is* such a thing as too much of a good thing.

Say what?

Let's go back to animal training again. If an animal trainer constantly uses the clicker when the animal does something correctly, but never follows it up with something tangibly rewarding to the animal like food or a toy, the animal will start to lose the motivation to complete the desired behavior. Eventually, performance begins to break down.

This happens with people too. Too much affirmation can lose impact when it isn't followed with more tangible rewards. Ridley Scott's affirmation was important, but if I hadn't been paid, too, I would soon have become "immune" to it.

A few years ago, I was watching a Little League baseball game. On one team, there was a father, who was one of the coaches, and his 10-year-old son. The little boy was a pitcher, and from the way it looked, he was very athletic—probably the best kid on the team.

It was one of the very first games of the season, and I noticed that the father talked to his son from the sidelines while he was on the pitcher's mound.

From the beginning of the first inning, after every pitch, the boy's father would shout to him. When a pitch was thrown over the plate, he would yell to the kid, "Great pitch!!" When the ball was thrown a little outside or inside, he would say, "You got to get it over the plate..." The guy made a comment after every pitch—I mean *every single pitch.*

I'm sure the father had good intentions, but despite how athletic and advanced this little kid was, I kept thinking that if the father continued the barrage, the kid would surely have a meltdown somewhere during the season.

It only took three weeks. The boy was pitching, and on this particular day, his aim was a little off. I heard his father trying to motivate him, once again trying to help him the way he always did. On this day, because the pitches were seldom going over the plate, all the kid heard, over and over, was, "YOU'VE GOT TO GET IT OVER THE PLATE!!"

By this time in the season, the little boy was *conditioned* to expect an affirmation coming from his father after every pitch, but now he no longer heard it.

Within two innings, it was obvious that the kid was struggling. His father tried to encourage him the few times he threw the pitch over the plate, but that didn't seem to help. So the father tried to help the kid even more, and the child began to ignore him. The more the father talked, the more the boy ignored his father, and the worse his attitude seemed to become. Before long, the kid was in tears, and a few innings later, the father pulled him out of the game.

So why did all this happen? Just as with animals, there is no question that humans need incentives, and a child even more at certain times, especially when in competition.

In this case, what do you think was the child's main motivation? What drove his desire to throw the pitch over the plate?

Several things came into play. One is the sheer heat of competition. Unlike dogs or marine mammals, people often compete with others in games, and the drive to win motivates us to succeed. Some people thrive on competition more than others, but competition can be healthy in many instances.

In this case, however, aside from his desire to win, the boy's primary drive for pitching well was getting his dad's approval. His legitimate, authentic approval.

That primary reinforcement is something that is very valuable, but it's also something that can be diluted if it's communicated the wrong way. It would have been great if the father's affirmations had come periodically and randomly, and *only* when the child threw a good pitch. But that's not what happened.

What did happen is that the affirmation came every time the child threw the ball, even when *the boy knew it wasn't over the plate*. With the father constantly telling the child he threw a good pitch each time the ball was thrown, the effectiveness of his attempts to encourage his son eventually became diluted. It would be a long time, if ever, before they served to inspire the kid again.

Let's go over that last part again.

We understood that the affirmation coming from the father was important for the child to hear, and that was essentially the child's primary reinforcement. However, because the constant affirmation came from the father on an almost regular basis, that reward that had, at first, meant so much to the child lost its impact. Once the reward lost the impact that it had once had, the child lost his motivation and good attitude.

Whether you're teaching kids or managing people, motivating always involves a primary reinforcement. Unfortunately, with adults especially, we don't always know what it is unless we understand the individual. Our primary motivations for doing well in school, on the playing field, or at work, vary. If you're the trainer or manager, it's important that you identify the primary reinforcers, and reward thoughtfully, so feedback about performance continues to be unique and geared to the particular person.

More About Competition

As I mentioned above, one of the things we humans uniquely do is compete for rewards. Though it too can be overemphasized, competition isn't unhealthy in and of itself. We all know of instances where people competing with each other brings out the best in both. As the person in charge, you have the ability to create an environment of healthy competition between people in the group you manage or teach.

The greatest thing about competition is that it can become "contagious" without any assistance from you. As employees or students observe positive traits in their co-workers and classmates—e.g., a good work ethic or the motivation to do well in school—and they see those traits rewarded, they often begin to emulate those behaviors. If students see other students receive certain accolades for getting good grades, might they not study a little harder? If you are a parent with two school-aged children, for instance, if one of them is rewarded for doing well in school, might not the other child be incentivized to achieve at his sibling's level?

Of course, many factors impact the self-esteem and motivation of humans, but generally speaking, if the environment is one in which all have a legitimate opportunity to achieve and earn a reward, healthy competition can bring out the best in everyone.

Facilitating Healthy Competition

How is healthy competition created? There are many ways this can be brought about, but one of them is for managers or teachers to publicly communicate to their reports and students when they're doing things correctly, and at times, rewarding those people for their efforts. If we're talking about an employee who's done something very well, and is receiving a reward for it, that reward might be an extra day off with pay, an increase in salary, or maybe even a promotion; at the very least, an adequate reward might be nothing more than that employee receiving the affirmation for the job done well. The effectiveness of the reward depends entirely upon the appropriate communication and its timeliness.

TEAMS

One difference between training animals and dealing with people is that animal training generally takes place one-on-one: when the animal does something correctly, he's rewarded individually. However, when a teacher is working with a group of individuals, the situation is much different, and can be even more fun. (The same thing is true for groups of employees, like project teams.)

Years ago, I was involved in training four Pacific "bottle-nosed" dolphins to jump over a rope. A rope was run across the entire width of a pool, and once the rope was in place, it was raised to a height of between six and ten feet.

As many of you have seen before, dolphins are often trained to go around the pool at the same time and gather speed. Then, they dive to the bottom before breaking the surface with a beautiful bow as they jump over the rope together.

Those dolphins are trained to perform as a team, and they are always rewarded and/or corrected as a team. In other words, if for some reason one of the dolphins fails to jump over the rope or hit the rope, not only would *that* dolphin not be rewarded, but neither will the other three.

It was amazing to me that it generally took only one dolphin messing up for them to get it right the next time. Somehow they communicated with each other while swimming at high speeds, positioned themselves perfectly and then together made the run prior to the jump!

If you're a teacher or manager, you can reward your students or reports as a group too. What's great about this is that once the group is rewarded as a team for their hard work, they're most likely to maintain a strong work ethic because they are now not only accountable to you, but to each other as well.

Another good thing about this is that when rewarded as a team, individuals stronger in one area will often help those who are weak in that area. Most importantly, though, as long as the opportunity is available to everyone, and each member of the team is rewarded or corrected in the same manner, you've provided a more positive and emotionally safe working environment.

If you're a teacher whose students do well working as a group, sometimes changing the order in which things are done during the school day can be reinforcing. And remember the concept of negative reinforcement? Occasionally give them a break from some of the tougher activities.

If you're managing people, the same thing can apply. Take a look at the work that some of the people are doing together as a team. When you see them working hard, find a way to change the routine once in a while. If they're paid a certain amount each week, and you have the authority to do it, you might pay them an unexpected bonus. Remember, too, that for most people, a paycheck isn't the only reward. Being told when they've done an exemplary job goes a long way.

Here are a few other relatively simple ideas for how to change things up. Keep in mind that rewards work best if they're given on a random basis.

- *Lunch hour increased from 1 hour to an hour and a half*
- *Half a day off following successful completion of a large or stressful project*
- *Extra small breaks throughout the day*
- *Taking them out for lunch on the company*
- *Scheduling a fun and unexpected activity for the group.*

If you are a parent and your kids are not getting along well, do something fun with your kids as a group. Watch for opportunities to positively reinforce them when they make an effort to get along together. Let them know how much you appreciate their working or playing together well.

CHAPTER 4
CORRECTION

Many of today's animal trainers focus too much and sometimes *only* on what happens when the animal they're working with does something *correctly*. But what about when an animal's behavior is not the one you want to elicit?

The truth is that this is more likely to be the situation than not, especially for new pet owners. At the beginning of training, a dog will generally do more things *wrong* than right, leaving the unprepared owner pulling out her hair.

How to reward for "good" behavior is easy to "get," but how a trainer or owner responds to an animal that does something *incorrectly* can have a huge impact not only on relationship-building with his pet, but also on how well and how quickly the animal begins to understand what it is that the trainer wants it to do. As I intimated above, it has been my experience that in order for an animal to understand how to do something *right*, he must first do it *wrong*.

And once again, humans are no different. When a person first attempts to do something you ask, it is not unusual for it to be not exactly the way you requested. (Consider learning to play a musical instrument or shoot a basketball.) And the learning process is not just for those you are training—guiding by correction requires that you hone your communication skills.

The first step in training an animal is in determining what is and what is not an acceptable behavior. Feedback that communicates which is which is essential to an efficient learning process. As a part of that process, an animal must be corrected when he doesn't meet the behavioral requirements of the trainer.

If when an animal behaves incorrectly, he isn't corrected, or when the correction technique is applied inappropriately, negative results can occur.

Consistency

It is essential that the animal understand that when he performs incorrectly, he will always be corrected *in the same manner*. This means that once determined to be effective with an animal, the technique used to correct undesired behavior will *always remain the same.*

Why do we not want to change the correction? BECAUSE CHANGE IS REINFORCING. As we talked about earlier, when a trainer changes something, it is reinforcing to the animal. If change is reinforcing (increasing the likelihood that the behavior will be repeated), then it only makes sense that changing the way we correct should be avoided.

Severity

You will remember that I avoid using the term "punishment" in animal training because we have come in popular culture to always think of punishment in a negative way. To my way of thinking, there is a big difference between correcting behavior and punishing it.

I have seen trainers use correction techniques that are way too severe for the behavior exhibited, and quite often, the corrections weren't physical in nature.

Here's where really knowing an animal is crucial.

For example, simply saying the word "no" in a normal tone of voice may be sufficient to correct a shy or fearful animal, and raising one's voice dramatically can hinder development of trust and the relationship you are trying so hard to build.

I've also seen situations where a correction had no impact at all. A correction needs to have some sort of effect on the animal, usually one that he or she wants to avoid. Simply put, if a correction has no impact, the animal never learns what is *not* expected of him. CONFUSION – What creates confusion in an animal? Poor training technique. Almost 100% of the time, if an animal is confused, the fault lies with the person training him. If an animal is corrected inconsistently for undesired behavior, with a correction appropriate for his temperament, he will never come to understand what is or what is not expected of him, and will often become resistant or fearful in training situations.

I can't say it enough. The best animal trainers are those who've learned how to give a correction, get the message across to the animal that the behavior was done incorrectly and move on without affecting the trust relationship between trainer and animal. This requires that the trainer really study the animal he's training.

Something that is more than adequate as a correction for one animal might not work as well for another, and giving the wrong correction to the wrong animal can lead to serious problems in trust, permanently jeopardizing the trainer's relationship with the animal.

The moral of the story? Fit the correction to the animal.

Corrections in Dog Training

Let's go over what we've learned about dog training so far. When training a dog, there are two things you always wants to be sure to do: 1) identify the most reinforcing thing the animal likes, and 2) give that reward to the dog when he does something correctly. As we talked about before, this might be something like a treat, a ball, a toy, scratching him in his favorite spot, or simply patting him on the head.

A skilled trainer also understands those times when the dog does something wrong, he is in need of correction. The trainer wants to be sure to use the most optimal means of correction for that particular animal for that specific situation at that particular moment. And to do it consistently.

Contrary to what some people in the animal training profession believe, correcting a dog neither hurts the animal nor destroys the animal's trust. Often, it is correction enough to not give the "expected" reward.

The most successful dog trainers also understand that the *completion* of an *undesired* behavior *is in itself a reward*. In other words, if we allow a "bad" behavior to occur without interruption, the very fact that the behavior is finished *reinforces* it. Here are a few examples:

- **Getting into the trash.** If a dog gets into the trash and nobody is there to stop him, will he do it again? Yes, if he doesn't know that he shouldn't. Having gotten into the trash, would he find something to eat? Probably. Would he eat it? Yes. Is food rewarding to a dog? Yes.
- **Relieves himself on the carpet.** If a dog relieves himself on the carpet when there's nobody there to

let him out, will he do it again? Yes. Does relieving himself on the carpet (or anywhere, for that matter) make him feel good? Absolutely. (Don't you feel better afterward?)

- **Jumps on guests.** Why does a dog jump on guests? In many instances, it's intent is to get closer to a guest's face or it's simply due to excitement. Does that make him feel good? Absolutely. So, if he is allowed to *complete* the behavior of jumping up on a guest, will he do it again? No doubt. Why wouldn't he do something again that made him feel good, something for which he was rewarded?
- **Chases or barks at the mailman.** If a dog barks at the mailman, it likely stems from the natural tendency of dogs to bark at unknown persons in their "territories." Because this person in uniform leaves when the dog barks, a pattern now develops. (The dog has no idea why the mailman leaves... just that he does.) Did it make the dog feel good? Absolutely. Do cars that drive by keep going? Yep. This is a very rewarding experience for a dog. What's worse is that the mailman's behavior is reinforced at least six days a week. Dog barks, intruder goes away. It's just like a rat pressing a bar. Press bar, food appears.

Let's take a further look at these examples.

In example one, we have a dog going into the trash. If you were to put a very long leash on the dog and let him make his way to the trash can, and then just before he got to the trash bag, if you were to correct him lightly and say the word "no," he would probably stop and look at you. You would have communicated to him exactly how he is to behave—he is to "stop short" of the trash. If, a few minutes later, you repeat the same thing, he would probably stop before the trash can and again look at you.

By repeating this scenario over the course of time, the animal learns that going toward the garbage can results in a non-reward—a correction.

In example number two, we have a dog relieving himself on the carpet. Why did the dog relieve himself on the carpet? He did it because relieving himself is reinforcing—it made him feel good. Once it happened, the behavior was completed. Nothing happened to discourage this behavior from taking place in the future unless the training starts over.

This is why the old "rolled-up newspaper thing" is crazy. Putting animal's nose in the mess or striking him is ridiculous, and an incredible waste of time. For one thing, it is guaranteed to destroy his trust in the person training him. Most importantly, it does NOT put the dog in a situation which provides him with the opportunity to start and complete the process. This is totally unproductive and more likely destructive.

In example number three, we have a dog jumping on guests. I did an entire episode on "untraining" this behavior on "GOOD DOG U" on Animal Planet. The dog jumps on the guests because for whatever reason, it makes him feel good to put his feet on them. We want the dog to understand that this is *not* acceptable behavior. If we put a long line on the dog and, just before he puts his feet on someone, we say the word "no" and correct him, we will get his attention. He will most likely be surprised, stop, and look at us. We will have communicated to him exactly what we want, that he is not to put his feet up on the guests. If, a few minutes later, we were to repeat the same thing, he again would probably stop and look at us, *interrupted* in his quest to put his feet up on the guest. (Remember, the goal of a correction is to NOT allow him to complete the jumping up behavior.)

Just as in the first example, you can see that by repeating the correction every time he does it, the animal learns that the impulse to jump up and put his feet on a person results in a non-reward.

The best trainers are the ones who are great at "balancing" things: they are able to positively reinforce the behaviors they want their "trainees" to exhibit, and sideline "bad" behavior by correcting the animal appropriately 1) at exactly the right time, 2) with the most appropriate correction, and 3) without jeopardizing their trust and relationship with the animal.

Just as some things that reinforce a behavior in one dog aren't rewarding to other dogs, effective corrections can vary just as much. What one person may use with one dog, others may not use. A dog that's very high strung might need more of a physical correction, but a small or timid dog might need less—perhaps nothing more than the trainer saying the word "no" very softly.

I have a problem with animal training methods that try to generalize about dog training, approaching every dog the same way. I can't say it enough: If a trainer uses the same correction for every animal, he will not be giving the best correction for some. Why?

That's right. Because all dogs are different.

Correction with Marine Mammals

Now, let's take a look at how this works in marine mammal training. Training marine mammals is, in some ways, a lot simpler because there are no physical corrections involved. Can you imagine trying to put a leash on a dolphin?

In this case, when an animal does something wrong, he's simply *not rewarded*, and most likely, the trainer will give him a chance to repeat the behavior again. Marine mammals often work together and all receive the same correction, while dog training generally involves one specific animal.

Even so, though the conditions are different, there are many ways in which the use of rewards and corrections are similar in training both species of animal.

Imagine that we have a dolphin that is given a cue to do a front flip. He leaves the trainer and goes out and does a beautiful back flip, and returns, expecting a reward. Unfortunately, even though it was a "great" back flip, *the dolphin did not do what the trainer asked him to do.*

If he rewards the dolphin, the dolphin has learned that it's OK to go out and do a back flip when given a cue for a *front* flip. Furthermore, rewarding the dolphin even once for an undesired behavior creates a lot of confusion for the animal.

In contrast, if the trainer does *not* reward the dolphin and asks him to repeat it again, he gives the animal another chance to perform the flip right. If the dolphin then goes out and does the behavior correctly, and is rewarded for performing the desired trick, the message has been clearly sent. "If you do a back flip when I give you the front flip cue, you will *not* be rewarded. However, if you do a front flip when I give you a front flip cue, you *will* be rewarded."

Now a scenario with a dog.

A trainer is working with a very shy dog that learned how to "stay" only a few weeks ago. He tells the dog to stay, but for whatever reason, the dog trots over to the trainer instead. The trainer gently takes the dog back to the spot where he was when the command was first issued and, once again, tells him to stay. The dog now stays.

What does the trainer do? He *walks to the dog* and rewards the dog *on the spot where he is responding with the correct behavior*, in this situation, "staying."

If the trainer were not to require the dog to repeat the behavior, the dog would have learned not to "stay" but that it is OK in response to the command to stay to come to the trainer. The trainer will simply repeat this until the dog *does what the trainer asked of him.*

Here is one final example of using a correction in *dog* training where I let the dog "figure things out." This principle comes directly from my experiences in marine mammal training.

In the photo on the next page, we see my dog Foster standing with his front feet on a piece of cardboard. Almost all dogs who work in movies, on TV shows, and in commercials are trained using this behavior. The piece of cardboard is called a "mark," and you can place it anywhere on the set so the dog can put his front feet on it. As the dog becomes accustomed to performing using a mark, it becomes smaller and smaller in size until it FADES down to something as insignificant as a piece of tape on the ground. Directors love it because the camera doesn't "see it" and, just as with an actor, the dog knows exactly where to go.

Foster standing on a "mark," a piece of cardboard he can put his front feet on.

In the initial stages of training to a mark, I use a technique I learned in marine mammal training. Here's how it works. In the photo below, Foster is standing 12 inches behind the "mark."

The goal is simply to train Foster to put his front feet on the mark. (Note that we are not training him to go to particular places in a room, just to the mark.) Once we guide Foster to the mark and he puts his front feet on it, as he does in in the photo below, he has completed the behavior I want him to do.

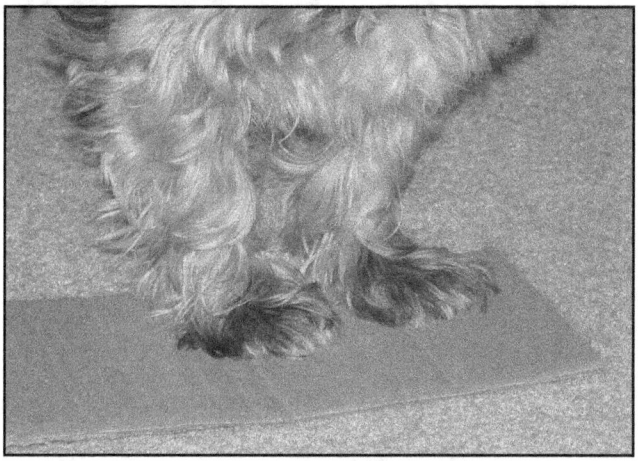

Foster standing on a "mark.

As Foster comes to understand that he is to go to the "mark," I begin to back away from him until I'm standing about two feet in front of it.

Here's where the dog will start to make some mistakes. The next time I give him the cue to go to the "mark," one of two things will happen:

- *he will either stop with his front feet on the "mark," or*
- *he will overshoot it as you can see in the photo on the top of the next page.*

I will correct him by taking him back to his original position, and once again telling him "mark." If he overshoots it

Bond With Your Heart...Train With Your Brain

Foster misses the "mark," with his feet in front of, not on the cardboard.

again, I will repeat bringing him back to his original position. After the second or third try, he will stop on the "mark" on his own and be reinforced for it.

What I've done is let him "figure it out." I wait for him to accidentally or otherwise perform the correct behavior. I want him to learn to stop on the "mark," not because I said "no" or told him to stop.

This is a classic style of basic marine mammal training, because there's no real way to "correct" except not to reward. If you think about if from the dog's point of view, it could not be more positive—there is no need for either physical correction or my saying the word "no." I require the dog to repeat the behavior until he stops where I want him to.

What *some* trainers (usually those without experience in marine mammal training) will do, as the dog overshoots it, is say "no" and tell the dog to back up until it *backs up* onto the "mark." And *then* they reward the dog. But what behavior are they actually rewarding him for? *The entire chain of events*, which includes 1) overshooting the "mark," 2) backing up, and 3) *then* stepping on the "mark."

If the trainer continues this sequence, the dog will learn not to go straight to the mark, but to overshoot it and back up because *that's what he's been rewarded for.*

People

Once again, because people are animals, too, we are very much the same. We develop "bad" behavior patterns, and if they're practiced, which is not only rewarding for completion, but reinforced, they can grow into bad behavior patterns that become ingrained. But if they're caught early on and corrected...

Here's an example of an "incorrect" behavior pattern I personally developed.

When I was learning to type, I consistently mixed up the "O" key and the "I" key. I mixed them up so much that it became a *habit*. I was aware that I kept making the mistake, but I still continued to do it.

What was I doing? Hitting the "O" key, then the "BACKSPACE" bar, and then the "I" key, or vice versa. Completion of the "bad" behavior resulted in my developing the habit of repeating the sequence instead of fixing the problem.

So what did I do? I went back to the things I know about animal training. I realized that my typing "faux pas" was really no different from giving a dog the opportunity to complete a "bad" behavior, like jumping up on guests. Just as with the dog in our earlier discussion, I allowed myself to start the process (an incorrect chain of events) and complete it, and my behavior "problem" continued until I *stopped letting the chain of events begin.* Here's how I *corrected* my typing misbehavior.

When I knew that I needed to type an "O," I would stop for a brief second and ensure that I hit the proper key from the beginning. I would do the exact same thing when I needed to hit the "I" key, as well.

By taking these small steps, *I no longer gave myself the opportunity to press the wrong key.* Once I stopped entering the sequence of negative events, the mistyping quit happening.

Communication vs. Correction

Remember the story in the last chapter, about the baseball coach and his 10-year-old son? Out of force of habit, he would say, every time, "You need to get it over the plate."

When I heard it, I thought of *my* father, who would have said to him: "Do you think the kid doesn't *know* he needs to throw the ball over the plate?"

Was the father really intending to correct the child or was he just trying to communicate with him? We know the true answer to that question. He wasn't trying to correct his son, because it wouldn't have been possible to address problems with pitching mechanics with any success in the middle of a game.

Did the father's almost constant communication help his son? How much did the communication actually mean to the child at the time?

If the father's comments had been made unpredictably, and occasionally, there would have been no harm done. There are a number of ways he might have successfully gotten across what he meant to communicate, and might have had a huge positive impact, giving the son encouragement and extra motivation to succeed.

But because it happened over and over again, what the father was saying began to lose impact. The child not only stopped listening to what his father was saying, but could no longer benefit from his guidance.

Because I'd seen the same thing happen with animals, it was unfortunately no surprise to me when the child had a "meltdown" during the third game of the season.

When we "correct" another person, we usually intend to help him or her improve at some task, a simple means of helping them "get it right" the next time.

What might the father have done differently?

First of all, there is *always* a reason someone gets something wrong, but people are very complex, and without adequate time and focus, we can't always determine the reason.

But one thing is sure. The reason the boy wasn't getting the ball over the plate was *not* because he wasn't *trying*. There were any number of things he might have been doing incorrectly: his windup may have been too fast, he might have been trying to throw the ball too hard, he may not have been bringing his arm back far enough before he threw it, or he may have been concentrating on a runner on second base.

The point is that any one of those (and a host of others I didn't mention) may have been source of the problem, but unless the father could identify *what the problem was at the time*, he couldn't have given the child an *appropriate* correction during the game. He could certainly have communicated better with the boy in order to have helped motivate him, but quite often communication and correction can be totally different things. They can be easily misinterpreted by the person being trained; instead of feeling encouraged, the child was more likely *dis*couraged.

When the father begins to understand the difference between communication and correction, as well as the appropriateness of timing, and *if he knows his child*, he will figure out that during a game he needs to encourage and support his son when he throws a bad pitch (and everyone will, even in the major leagues). That is *communicating*.

If he sees a pattern of something the child is doing that may be contributing to his problem, he can take a few seconds to talk to him about it between innings. Preferable to that would be saving it for practice time, when the pressure of competition isn't a factor. That is *correcting*.

People

As I've said more than once, as with animals, all people are different, and with people there's a lot more variation. Some people respond differently from others to the same corrections. A correction you use with one child, for instance, may not be effective with another.

It is essential that you use the right correction technique for each person. As you heard me say in the beginning and will hear me say again and again, in order to be able to do this, you must make the time for developing trusting relationships by getting to know your workers or students well.

Unfortunately, it is apparent that not enough people take the time to get to know the people they're supervising or teaching, or make the mistake of not seeing how important it is.

The bottom line is that different people are motivated by different things and different people interpret corrections in different ways. The only way to increase your probability of success in motivating positive action or correcting maladaptive behaviors, in the classroom or workplace, is to know your individual students or employees.

If you remember nothing else from this chapter, remember this: THE COMPLETION OF A "BAD" BEHAVIOR IS, IN ITSELF, A REWARD. Correction is, very simply, not allowing the bad behavior to take root.

People, just like animals, are going to make mistakes. It's part of being human and it's how we learn. By taking the time to get to know the people that you're working with, you can choose the best way to correct behavior based on consideration for them as individuals.

Remember, also, as you read in Chapter 3, that CHANGE IS REINFORCING. Once you've determined what is the best correction technique for a person, *make sure that the way you correct him or her always remains the same*. When you change your way of correcting, especially with children, you can actually reinforce negative behaviors without even realizing it.

As a teacher, trainer or manager, it's up to you to communicate to your employees, workers, or students the limits outside of which their behavior cannot go while they are under your direction.

We humans are pretty intelligent creatures, and like Foster, no matter how long it may take, we'll figure it out,

CHAPTER 5
MARINE MAMMAL BEHAVIOR

At places like Sea World, marine mammals do some amazing things. But what the average observer doesn't see is that the most difficult, most complex behaviors marine mammals are trained to perform are little more than just a series of completed goals. Training a dolphin, for example, to exhibit a series of behaviors in sequence involves systematic steps, and many very small approximations toward the desired behaviors. Small steps are also part of getting the best out of your children, employees or students, too.

Marine Mammal Training is Always Positive

One of the primary reasons I liked marine mammal training is that successful training techniques used with large sea animals always involves reinforcement. There is virtually no way to effectively train a marine mammal using "punishment" approaches. (It's not like you can spank a whale or physically correct it in any way.)

Think about a show with a sea lion or a dolphin you may have seen in a theme park or oceanarium. Didn't you almost always see the trainer relating to the animals in a positive way with food or some other type of reward, like petting them?

Whatever reward you may have seen used, the positive response let the animals know that whatever they did was acceptable, and was probably also a way of simply communicating with them—fun for both trainer and animal.

From 1981 to 1987, I trained a wide variety of marine mammals and in 1986, won the "Behavior of the Year" award from the International Marine Animal Trainers Association (IMATA) for a "trick" I trained two Atlantic bottle-nosed dolphins to perform.

It involved my diving into the pool with the dolphins, having the dolphins "push" me with their noses to the bottom and then, each with a nose under one of my feet, come back up and out of the water. The trick ended with all of us involved in a jump, breaking through the water surface and then diving back in together.

There are many differences between marine mammal and dog training, but there are many similarities, too. The most important one to me is that *once a relationship is developed*, both types of animals will look to you for guidance.

Because of two-way nature of the relationship, the knowledge and sense of the individual animal you're working with is your greatest asset. Sometimes the body language of an animal will let you know how it's feeling. (We'll talk about *our* body language as trainers later.)

Take a dog for instance. When he is excited to see you, he will most likely run over to you and put his feet up on you to greet you.

A sea lion, on the other hand, will come charging out of the water, slide across the stage area on his stomach, stopping in front of you with his nose in your face.

A dolphin might just bob up and down in the water, resting his "chin" on the stage, or jump out of the water in his excitement at seeing you. These are all simple signs of the animal wanting to be around the owner or trainer, ready to learn.

In general, marine mammals are curious, creative, and *very* innovative. There are times when *they* create brand new behaviors all on their own. This adds a lot to their personality and enhances training. As the trainer, you don't always have to come up with new ideas—you can sometimes just let them be creative and do literally whatever they want.

Using Natural Socialization in Training

No matter what kind of animal we are training, much of what we expect them to do is based on the animal's natural way of life. For example, marine mammals are social animals, and this is something that can be used to your advantage. Most trainers find that marine mammals, just like dogs, like to interact with people and each other. If an animal would rather be with another animal or group of animals than by itself, you can make training it with others a reward.

The nature of socialization varies among different types of marine mammals as well as between different individual animals—like people, some are more sociable than others.

With the California sea lion, for example, sometimes just being in the same pool with another California sea lion can be rewarding enough. (Sometimes it's not just a sea lion, but a specific other California sea lion, too.) In the wild, sometimes you see hundreds of sea lions hauled out on the rocks sleeping together!

With dolphins and whales, quite often you'll see them swimming together and sometimes playing or chasing each other around. If you go to a theme park, almost all the time you will even see "a few" killer whales or dolphins swimming around in a pool together—most of the time, they come up at the exact same time for breaths of air. They naturally choose to be around each other.

People are very much the same. Much of the social behavior I've seen with marine mammals happens in groups of people, too. If you have a group of employees or students, and you just introduce them to one another, groups will begin form.

And what you will find, quite naturally, that certain types of people like being around the *same* types of people. If a student would rather sit next to, and talk to another student, there is probably a reason for it. If an employee would rather work with another employee, it's probably because he likes being around the other employee.

With rewards and corrections relating to appropriate behavior (namely, if the jobs they are hired to do get done or their behavior in the classroom is acceptable), more can sometimes be accomplished when people feel comfortable with their co-workers and classmates.

Training with Targets

Training an animal that can come out of the water and walk on land is much easier than training an animal that lives only in the water. (The obvious reason for this is that when an animal can get out on land, you can stand right next to it. These include the California sea lion, the walrus, North American river otters, Malaysian short clawed river otters, and sea otters.)

But that fact takes nothing away from the experience of training of dolphins and whales, though. In all my years of training, the killer whale has always been my favorite, and the most fun to me to train. My only regret is that I had the opportunity to train killer whale in my early twenties. Now, in my mid to late forties, I would appreciate their intelligence and power much more than I did then.

Whether they're on land or in the water, the most important tool in the toolkit for training marine mammals is what is known as a "target."

A target is nothing more than a long stick with a ball on the end of it. You may have seen trainers at parks pull one out at one time or another. An example is shown in the photo below.

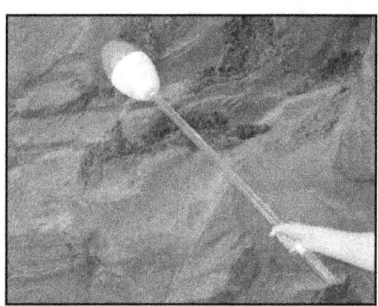

A target can be made from a variety of things, including your fist, and can vary in length from one to 12 feet depending on the animal and environment.

The message to a marine animal is simply this: "Touch your nose on the ball at the end of the stick and you will get a reward." That's all it is! Believe it or not, regardless of the behaviors you see marine mammals perform in theme park shows, they were first trained using a target.

And the greatest thing about training with targets is that is the process is 100% *positive.*

Sea Lions

Before we get into a discussion about the training of sea lions, I need to get something off my chest. The animals that you see performing in shows balancing balls on their noses are *not* seals, as many people think. They are *sea lions*, and almost all of them are *California* sea lions.

One of the biggest differences between seals and sea lions is that sea lions are able to rotate their hind flippers under their bodies and, at the same time, support themselves with their long and leathery-looking front flippers. They move around very well on land, and can get going very fast if they need to.

Seals, on the other hand, *cannot* rotate their hind flippers under their bodies and have *tiny* front flippers, so they are able only to undulate on land like a worm. When swimming, the sea lion uses the up and down motion of his front flippers, almost like a bird, to gain very fast speeds. A seal uses a slower side-to-side motion like that of a fish.

Another difference has to do with ears and vocal cords. A sea lion has an earflap over its ear "hole," where a seal has only the hole. Also, sea lions have vocal cords and are able to make those loud obnoxious barking noises you've probably heard. Seals, on the other hand, lack vocal cords, and make only grunting sounds.

Understanding all of that, you can see why we choose to train sea lions for shows—they're more entertaining in the end. But I've always thought the best part about training sea lions is their natural attitudes. Trainers who've been around a while call them "sea *dogs*," which is a great nickname, because, like dogs, they're extremely social animals with an incredible appetite (literally), and a strong desire to learn.

An average sea lion eats from 15 to 30 lbs. of fish every day. Because of this, trainers distribute food throughout the day in the form of training sessions, shows, or times of "free feeding."

The table below gives an example of how food may be rationed out each day. Because of the sea lion's high natural food drive, fish is almost always used as a reward; because sea lions like a variety in their diets, trainers will use a variety of fish as well. When I was working, we used squid, mackerel, herring, and smelt, the sea lions' favorites.

Animal	11:30 show	Training Session 1	2:30 Show	Training Session 2	TOTAL
Spunky	4 lbs.	3 lbs.	4 lbs.	3 lbs.	14 lbs.
Sammy	5 lbs.	4 lbs.	4 lbs.	2 lbs.	15 lbs.
Harry	7 lbs.	5 lbs.	5 lbs.	4 lbs.	21 lbs.

When the trainer uses one main thing to reward an animal with, it is called the *primary reinforcement*. Sea lions certainly like being around people, but the truth is *fish* are their paychecks. That is really what the sea lion works for. Fish are the primary reinforcement for that group of animals, just as food or food treats are the primary reinforcement for dogs.

The difference in dog training, though, is that once the dog is trained to perform the behavior on cue, we begin to fade out the food rewards, and increase the use of a tactile reward, like petting him. This way the dog eventually learns not to expect a food reward. With a sea lion, the food is consistently used throughout as the primary reinforcement.

In parenting, supervising employees, or teaching students, it is essential to remember that you and your "approval" are primary reinforcers. Your kids, your employees, and your students ultimately do the things they do for you, and not for a treat or a game.

Obviously, we can't give pats on the back every time someone does something good, nor do people expect it, but it's important to identify when they exceed expectations by acknowledging the fact.

Before I get into more specifics about training marine mammals, I want to give special thanks to the Shedd Acquarium in Chicago and their training staff for the use of their facility. All of the photos of marine mammals and training demonstrations you will see in the next few pages were taken there.

If you've never been to the Shedd Acquarium and you are in the Chicago area, be sure to visit. It is truly one of the most beautiful indoor marine mammal parks in the United States and I highly recommend it.

Other Training Techniques

I have always liked training techniques that allow for gentle manipulation. An example is that of holding a sea lion's flipper and gently moving it over his eye. (The finished behavior gives the appearance that the sea lion is hiding his eyes.)

Similarly, with dogs, to teach a dog to cover his eye, you can begin by gently placing the animal's paw over his eye, which familiarizes him with the behavior you want him to perform. Gentle manipulation of flippers and paws give animals the opportunity to understand what the trainer wants, especially when the desired behavior is *unlikely* to be performed otherwise.

Let's talk about how the "trick" of a sea lion covering his eyes is trained from scratch.

After getting the sea lion in a place that is stationary, the first step is to get him on a seat and begin the process of "targeting" on the trainer's fist. This is shown below.

"Targeting" on the fist is the same exact behavior as having the sea lion touch his nose to the ball on a stick. It is one of the first and easiest behaviors most trainers teach sea lions to do.

What's great is that once this basic behavior is trained, it gives a trainer a lot to build on. Wherever the trainer moves his fist, the sea lion will follow. (This is especially handy if the trainer wants the sea lion to walk next to him.)

So, when being taught, ultimately, to "cover his eyes," the sea lion learns first to touch his nose to the trainer's fist, and is rewarded for that.

The next step is to teach the sea lion to touch his *flipper* to the trainer's hand. As you can see below, the trainer reaches and simply touches the sea lion's flipper with his right hand, and rewards the sea lion *only* for that.

After a few training sessions, because he's so coordinated with his flipper, the sea lion will raise it a few inches to meet the trainer's hand, *just before the trainer moves to touch it.*

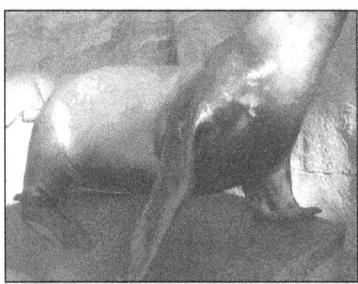

This we call "offering" a behavior. When an animal "offers" a behavior, it's something trainers like to see, because it tells the trainer that the animal "understands" what he wants; the animal initiates the behavior himself.

Once the sea lion understands that he will be rewarded for touching his flipper to the trainer's hand, the trainer will raise his hand, requiring that the sea lion raise his flipper a little higher.

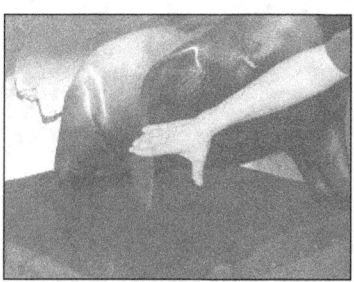

Once the sea lion is trained to touch the trainer's hand with his flipper, it doesn't take long for him to figure out to start raising his flipper a little higher to meet the trainer's hand earlier in the process and get his reward. You can see this here.

As the sea lion starts raising his flipper higher, the trainer now puts his hand closer to the sea lion's *face*, so that the sea lion will begin to touch his own face.

Because his front flippers are so large, when a sea lion touches his face, it appears that he is covering his eye.

Once the sea lion consistently performs that behavior, the trainer adds a unique verbal and visual "cue." Now the sea lion begins to associate the behavior of touching his flipper to his face with a verbal or visual cue.

And once *that* happens, training the sea lion to "cover his eye" in response to a cue is complete.

The moral of the story is that training a sea lion to cover his eye doesn't happen in one step. Instead, it is the result of a series of sequential steps, beginning with targeting on the trainer's fist.

Otters

Though otters are marine animals, they are much like opossums in that they have long bodies, shorter legs, and are able to scurry around on land very comfortably. In some instances, they're able to be gently "manipulated" into positions just like sea lions and dogs. However, just as with other marine mammals, only positive reinforcement techniques are used.

Three types of otters perform in the shows in many of the theme parks you might have been to. The smaller one is called a Malaysian Short-Clawed River Otter, the much larger one is the North American River Otter. A third, least commonly used in theme parks, is called a sea otter. As the name suggests, sea otters live in the ocean and come primarily from the coast of California. (These are the otters that you will see in the next few pages.)

As with sea lions, the fist target comes in handy for training sea otters too.

Teaching an Otter to Rear Up on Its Hind Legs

Because their bodies are so long and their legs so small, one of the cutest things that otters do is rear up on their hind legs.

Teaching an otter to perform this behavior on cue is a perfect example of how trainers take things that animals naturally do, build on it, and create a more complex trained behavior.

Sometimes the funniest thing about training this behavior is that different otters walk on their hind legs in different ways. One otter may walk on his hind legs in "expected" ways, others get into such a hurry to get to the trainer, they'll "hop" to get to him faster, and hopping becomes the trained behavior instead of walking.

In any case, what's the first thing trainers do when teaching otters to walk on their hind legs?

That's right. They "target" the otters to their fists.

Once the otter has learned to target to the fist, the trainer will raise her fist, as with the sea lions. In order for the otter to continue to target on the trainer's fist, he must rise up slightly.

Unlike sea lions, however, otters are very coordinated when standing on their hind legs, so learning proceeds quickly. Once an otter understands that he gets a reward for *slightly* rising up on his hind legs, the trainer raises her fist even a little higher.

Incrementally, the trainer raises her fist until successfully targeting requires that the otter stand up fully and comfortably. A verbal or visual cue is substituted for the fist, and once the animal stands up consistently on cue, the behavior is now trained.

Felix

I've lost some very special animal friends along the way, and Felix, a Malaysian short-clawed river otter, was one of them. Anyone who ever worked with this very unique otter knows that Felix was a special animal, and she (yes, Felix was a she) had a great life.

Felix performed in some of the shows I worked in. Unfortunately, she wasn't the smartest otter, but she loved to be held. Her favorite place to be was down inside your shirt.

It was really funny because she made noises like a human baby. The only problem is that otters are almost always wet and have a very musky smell. At lunch, you always knew who had been holding Felix earlier in the day, and more often than not, it was me. If she went down your shirt, you smelled like otter for the rest of the day.

The point of this story, of course, is the overall point of this book—that the relationship is the key. Even animals for whom food is usually a primary reinforcement develop connections to their trainers and vice versa. Felix was one of the most affectionate animals I have ever worked with, and I miss her to this day.

Training Marine Mammals in the Water

The most often trained mammals that live in water are dolphins and whales. Among those I've worked with are Pacific and Atlantic bottle-nosed dolphins, Pacific white-sided dolphins, beluga whales, pilot whales, and killer whales.

As you've seen, the most common first step in training animals on land is to train them to target on our fists. But how do we train if the animal is in the water...and we're not?

You may remember that I said a true "target" is a large stick with a small ball on the end of it, resembling a huge Q-tip®. With marine mammals, that target works just like the fist target used with sea lions and otters—acting almost like an extension of our arms.

Marine animals are first trained to touch their noses to the little ball on the end of the stick and learn that they will be rewarded for that. And over the course of time, just as with animals on land, the target becomes a key tool in training the animal to do other more complex things.

For instance, if you want an animal to move his head from side to side, you start by moving the target from side to side. After repeating this process over and over, the trainer adds a verbal or physical "cue." As he does that, he fades out the side-to-side motion of the target, replacing that stimulus with the cue.

As the animal begins to respond more and more to the cue, the trainer continues to fade out the use of the target until the animal responds by moving his head in a side to side motion *without* the use of the target. The behavior is now trained.

Training Dolphins to Bow

The dolphins you will see here are Pacific white-sided dolphins. These are smaller faster marine mammals found off the coast of California, and because of their energy and attitude, they are a blast to train!

One of the most basic of all aerial behaviors is what are called *bows*. A bow is nothing more than jumping up out of the water and re-entering the water head first.

To begin training a dolphin to bow, what do we do first? That's right. Before we even start to train on the desired behavior, we make sure the dolphin understands and responds to a target.

As we begin training, we use a target that is only a few feet in length. The first task is to train the dolphin to follow the target and then put his nose on it, as with other animals.

If you look at the photo at the top of the next page, we see that now the dolphin has his nose on the target and is perpendicular to it.

In the next pictures, the trainer presents the target a little higher. The dolphin reaches for the target, touches it and is rewarded.

The next step in this behavior is to train the dolphin to reach even a little higher for the target, which requires him to get even farther out of the water. When the dolphin jumps up and reaches for the target, by nature, he will re-enter the water nose first, completing the desired final behavior.

Once the dolphin performs the behavior consistently, the trainer now begins to transfer the behavior to another "cue." (Remember that up to now, the trainer has been using a physical target.)

The next step is one where a trainer "taps" the target in the water *in the exact area from where she wants the dolphin to jump out* of the water. The original trainer will give the animal a specific unique visual cue, and another will tap the target in the desired area. As the dolphin adjusts its behavior, the trainers will simultaneously fade out the use of the target. Once this process is complete, the dolphin has learned not only to bow, but that he must perform the bow in a specific area of the pool.

You may be wondering how teaching a dolphin to take a bow or a sea lion to cover his eyes relates to helping you get the best out of your employees or students?

The answer is twofold: 1) by reinforcing in you the importance of setting and communicating clear expectations for performance (goals) and 2) by remembering that all humans, including ourselves, don't learn complex things all at once. We learn in chunks, or small steps.

The dolphin didn't learn to "take a bow" overnight... neither did the sea lion learn to cover his eyes, nor the otter to rear up on his hind legs on command.

These are all very complex behaviors trained over the course of time, by trainers astute in how to break down a complex task into manageable chunks; they ensure that each "building block" is sufficiently mastered before moving on to the next. When their "trainees" achieved successful performance of each approximation or small behavior/goal, they moved on to the next one, by raising the standards or expectations and slowly changing the cues—from the target to verbal or visual signals.

By the time we reach "school age," most necessary human behaviors are complex in nature, so the same strategies we use in training marine mammals apply.

If you are a teacher with a group of students, set specific goals for learning, and plan activities as building blocks that allow for your students to acquire the skills they need to achieve the final goal.

If you are a manager of a group of employees, you and they are often faced with deadlines and requirements to get certain things done in a specific time period. First, define the ultimate outcome desired for yourself and those working for you; next, break the tasks into sequences of things that must be accomplished in order; and finally follow the plan to its completion. (You may notice that project planning software requires you to do those very things. It isn't an accident.)

If you are a parent, and your child has been having some problems in school, set a series of very achievable goals for him or her, celebrate each achievement, *rewarding in a way that fits your child*, and then "raise the bar" incrementally until the larger goal is accomplished.

Just as in marine mammal training, it's important to remember to give your kids, employees, or students the opportunity to *do complete things that are, in fact, achievable* in sequences you can reward at each step of the way.

Once they attain those goals, do it again. Build on that learning by setting different and sometimes increasingly more complex goals. I guarantee you'll be happy with the results!

CHAPTER 6
PREDICTABILITY

What do I mean by predictability? How is it defined in the animal training business? In general terms, if a situation is predictable, we "know" what will happen, what a person will do, *before* he does it.

The simplest example of this is the classical conditioning paradigm, originating with "Pavlov's dog." You may remember that the animal began to salivate when a bell rang because it had learned to associate the sound with the presentation of food, but this association only happened *because the pairing of the bell and food happened over and over again.*

The animal, consequently, began to "learn" from that series of events. What happened when the bell rang (food came) had become *predictable*.

You open a can with an electric can opener every single day, and then you put the food into a bowl and feed your cat. What happens when the cat hears the can opener? Why? Because the cat "knows" you will be dishing out its food into a bowl and soon.

The development of this routine didn't happen overnight, though. It occurred over the course of time. The very first time you opened the cat food with the can opener, the cat didn't come, did it?

Here's another example. You have a dog. Every time you are about to take it for a walk, you grab the leash from where it's hanging and walk to the front door.

As you walk from where the leash is to the front door, is your dog just casually hanging out in the house or following you happily, perhaps excitedly to the door? If he heard or saw you get the leash, the answer is yes. Just as it is with the cat, your dog has learned over time that when you retrieve the leash from its regular place, you are going to take him for a walk.

In the world of animal training, "predictability" is an event initiated by the trainer (often through things he or she may not even be aware of) occurring repeatedly or in some sort of sequence. The animal in training, over the course of time, learns to anticipate those events. Animals learn "cues" whether we intend for them to or not. The association of behaviors *will* happen, most notably when an animal is rewarded at the time the cue from the trainer occurs.

Although *all* learning necessarily begins with "predictable" behavior on the part of the trainer, the reality is that after the initial period of training, it can work in either a positive or negative way.

Trainers consciously dictate and are responsible for the way learning events unfold over time, but we may reinforce behaviors or reduce the effectiveness of rewards without even realizing it.

"If I do this, this happens. If I do that, that happens. If I do something else, nothing happens." Most intelligent animals and people possess the ability to perceive patterns that develop in their environments over the course of time, though they're not necessarily conscious of it. That's how we learn how to behave or in some cases, *not* behave. The proof is in the predictability—no pattern emerges without a certain amount of it.

Unfortunately, sometimes as trainers, we accidentally reinforce behaviors we don't intend to, facilitating the perception of unexpected patterns (it's unexpected to *us*, at least...) When problems result from predictable situations, they most likely originate from the person in charge, the one who is "calling the shots," whether a parent, teacher, manager, supervisor, or animal trainer.

Predictability *Can* Work in a Positive Way

As an example, let's use a dog that has been trained to "sit." If, for the last three weeks, all I have taught my dog to do is sit, and every time he sits, he is rewarded with something he likes, do you think he will sit? Of course, he will. Would you be surprised if sometime during that three-week period the dog begins to sit *even before I ask him to*? No surprise, huh. The reason is that he's learned that he has received that reward *every* times he sits. That's predictability. Think about it one more time:

- *The dog learned, over the course of time, that he would be rewarded each time he "sat."*
- *The dog learned that the only time he was rewarded with the treat was when he sat..*
- *Because he wants to receive the reward, the dog began to sit even before I gave him the cue.*

In specific circumstances, predictability can work in a very positive way for the trainer because the dog has the attitude that causes him to now "offer" behaviors. When an animal begins to offer behaviors, it is not only a sign of predictability, but it also indicates to the trainer that the animal is in such a good place that he looks forward to learning!

One of my very first jobs was working in a theme park in live shows at Universal Studios in Hollywood, California. During that time, we used animals such as dogs, birds, and cats that had previously been trained for movies, TV shows, and commercials.

The most impressive part of the show was the beginning, when we brought out "Fred," the cockatoo from the "Baretta" TV series. (Told you it was a long time ago.) We used a few different birds in the act, but the "actual" Fred also performed in the show. The bird performed many behaviors over a three-minute period of time, and was rewarded with a seed each time he did a behavior "right."

To this day, in all my years of performing with animals in live shows, this was by far one of the most efficient, smoothest and consistent sequences of behaviors. The bird rarely messed up, and the cockatoo performing in that show did thousands more shows than I ever did.

Now, why was this bird so consistent with a pattern in a show that never changed? Because some animals respond extremely well in predictable circumstances. They thrive in situations where what happens is consistent. From what I've seen, birds enjoy that.

While I don't mean to diminish the entertainment that birds provide, their brains are much smaller and "simpler" than the complex brains of dogs or dolphins. Because of this, I believe that some of the simpler creatures like birds are totally "content" with a set sequence that does not change. More complex animals, on the other hand, with a wide repertoire of behaviors, will often get bored.

Predictability and Marine Mammals

Every summer, we did many live shows with dolphins, sea lions, and killer whales—as many as 16 "sea lion shows" a day, with three sets of animals. Because that left no time to train the animals between the shows, the same show sequence was performed 16 times a day.

I mentioned above that if you reward a dog for sitting and *only* sitting, he will tend to begin sitting *before* you offer the reward. Do you think if you're asking extremely intelligent animals like sea lions to perform the same sequence of 50 or 60 behaviors over the course of 20 minutes every day for three months, they might begin to anticipate some behaviors? Of course, he will. This is what leads them into what is called "jumping" cues.

"Jumping" Cues

The tendency to "jump" cues results from predictability, particularly with marine mammals. As the name suggests, it simply means the animal "jumps ahead," and begins to do the behavior before the trainer gives him the cue.

Why does this happen? Because the animal wants the reward and, knowing that he must do the behavior in order to receive that reward, he begins to "offer" the behavior "early."

From the animal's point of view, the sooner he completes the behavior, the sooner he'll be rewarded. It totally makes sense, but it's counterproductive in a show if a behavior occurs out of sync.

Where a lot of new marine mammal or new dog owners get into trouble is because they don't pick up on their animals' early tendencies to jump cues. If the trainer isn't paying attention, the animal will learn that it's acceptable to start a desired behavior *before* the cue is given. And, once he initiates that behavior, if you follow with a reward, he will start "jumping" cues for other behaviors as well.

It's easy for trainers to become predictable with animals in a theme park where the same show is performed on a daily basis and behaviors are performed over and over in the same sequence. The result is that the trainer loses control—and the animal is likely to dictate what happens and when in future shows or training sessions.

This predictability may also result in what is called "show discrimination." Animals will work really well in training sessions, but during a "show," they may begin to perform a behavior much differently. Two major problems can develop from animals demonstrating "show discrimination":

- *The trainer is motivated not to disrupt the flow of the show even if there is a behavior problem that should be addressed. Because it is crucial in training to correct with predictability, not correcting appropriately can lead to a breakdown in performance of the desired behavior.*
- *The animal begins to jump cues.*

I've been just as guilty as any other trainer of setting the stage for show discrimination. As I mentioned earlier, I recall times when I did as many as 16 sea lion shows in a day. On one occasion, a sea lion messed up on the "ball balance" trick (balancing a ball on his nose).

Over the course of a few days, the sea lion became steadily worse—dropping the ball more and more during the show.

What happened? I chose to keep the show going.

If I had stopped and sacrificed one of the shows in order to ensure the sea lion performed the ball balance trick correctly, it would not have become a problem. Nor would I have given the "bad" behavior a chance to escalate. But because I didn't want to disrupt the flow of the show, I became predictable, and really dug myself into a hole.

Dolphins

Let's say we're training a dolphin to jump out of the water performing a "bow." You will remember that this behavior involves the dolphin jumping out of the water and re-entering it head first.

The height of a jump is trained by blowing a whistle at the peak of the bow. After the bow, the dolphin returns to the trainer and is rewarded. The whistle lets the animal know the exact second it reaches the acceptable height.

Initially, a trainer might blow the whistle each time the dolphin jumps *approximately* to the desired height. During the training session, though, the trainer will become more selective about when he blows the whistle, making sure he rewards a bow made at the optimum height.

When the dolphin's bow is lower than the trainer thinks is acceptable, he or she will simply not blow the whistle. If the dolphin comes to the stage for a reward, the trainer will give him, instead, another cue, requiring the dolphin to repeat the behavior. When he is asked to repeat the behavior, the dolphin pretty much "knows" the reason why—the last bow wasn't acceptable.

The trainer is more successful when he does *not* reward the dolphin for a less acceptable behavior, and has him, instead, repeat the sequence until it is performed correctly.

Now, take this situation to a live show situation with that same dolphin. The dolphin responds to her cue with a very low bow. The trainer does not want to disrupt the show but instead of rewarding the dolphin inappropriately, he continues the show.

What happens then?

Remember that "negative" predictability occurs only with respect to *rewards. Correction* requires the dolphin to repeat the behavior until it's done right.

If the trainer moves on with the show and an incorrect behavior is allowed to happen in two or three shows in a row, there is a good chance that he will start to see the dolphin's "bow" begin to decrease in height.

Remember, completing even a "bad" behavior is rewarding.

Dolphins Swimming Around the Perimeter

If you've seen a dolphin show, you have probably seen them swim very rapidly along the perimeter or outside edges of the pool. Many types of dolphins and whales are trained to do this, but it is most common among the Atlantic and Pacific bottle-nosed dolphins and Pacific white-sided dolphins, because they are the fastest swimmers. It is quite impressive to watch.

Though the dolphin seems to be doing nothing more than swimming around the pool in circles, there is a lot more to it than that. The behavior needs a lot of training maintenance to keep the dolphins doing it correctly. When a trainer is predictable and rewards a dolphin for one revolution around the perimeter of the pool, the behavior will more than likely fall apart. I will show you why this can happen.

Let me first show you how this behavior is trained. As you can see below, there are two trainers. Trainer 1 will give the dolphin the cue. As he does this, Trainer 2 will tap her target on the water. Once the dolphin touches the target, he returns to Trainer 1 and is rewarded.

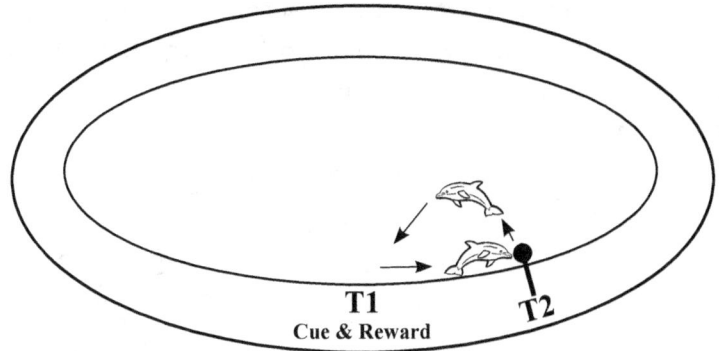

Once the dolphin understands this, another trainer positions himself a little farther away. When Trainer 1 gives the dolphin the cue, Trainer 2 taps his target on the water. Once the dolphin commits to the target and heads in that direction, she pulls it away, and Trainer 3 taps his target. Once the dolphin touches Trainer 3's target, he again returns back to the place he originally started, where it is again rewarded.

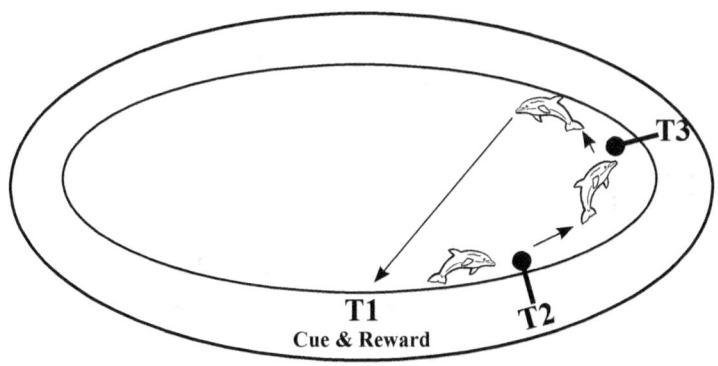

The next step is to bring in yet another trainer (T4) and position him as shown. As you can see, he is directly *across* the pool from the spot from which the dolphin will be starting. Based on what the dolphin has learned so far, he understands that once the cue is given, the first trainer will tap the target. Once the dolphin commits to it, the second trainer will tap *his* target. Once the dolphin commits to that target, T3 will tap *his* target. Once the dolphin touches the last target, he swims back to where he started, and is rewarded.

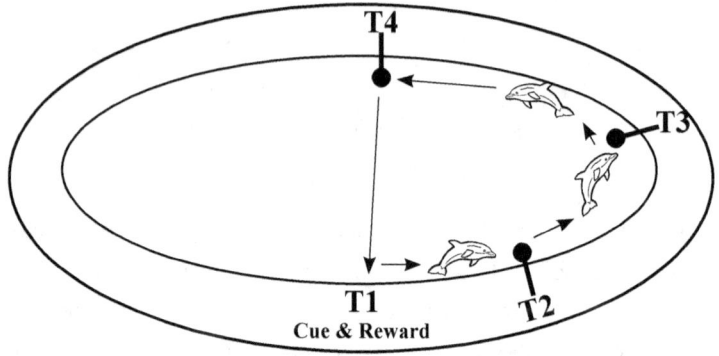

Training continues in this way until a trainer positioned ¾ of the way around the pool taps his target and then withdraws it.

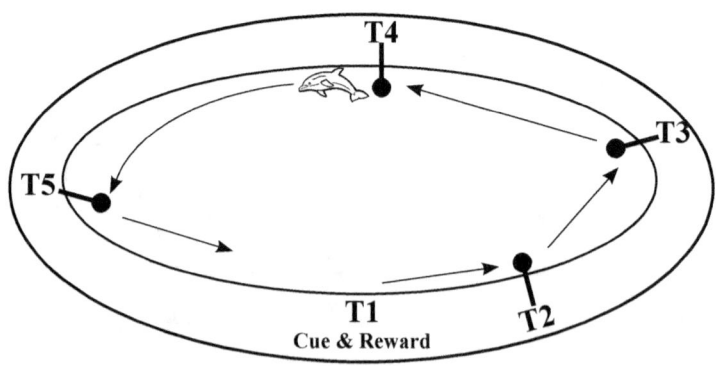

At this point, the *first* trainer will begin to tap *his* target. This time, the dolphin returns to the first trainer *not* for a reward, but *because he tapped his target*. When the dolphin touches that target, *then* he is rewarded for the whole behavior.

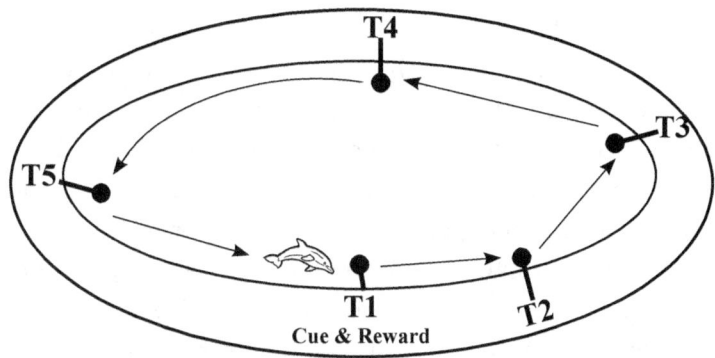

If we want the dolphin to begin a second revolution, all we need to do is position a trainer with a target as in Diagram 1. Then, we simply repeat what we did in order to train the behavior in the first place.

Once training the full behavior of swimming around the edge of the pool in a complete revolution is accomplished, we begin to systematically "fade out" trainers along the perimeter of the pool. In the best of training circumstances, the dolphin stays as close to the edge of the pool as possible when trainers are faded out. But not always…

Here's where predictability plays a key role.

Let's assume that in a show, a dolphin is rewarded for only one or two complete revolutions. Let's also assume that he's always (and only) rewarded by Trainer 1 (the trainer who gives the initial cue).

What you will see in the weeks to follow is that the dolphin begins to gradually swim farther and farther away from the sides of the pool, and more toward the center. In other words, over the course of time, the revolutions become smaller and smaller.

Why *is* this?

Think about it from the dolphin's point of view: If he knows that he is only rewarded at the center stage, why should he ever keep the circles close to the edges of the pool? In this scenario, the dolphin will *never* be rewarded at *other* places around the pool, and the behavior of swimming along the edge will most likely begin to disintegrate. It is, therefore, essential that the dolphin be rewarded at different times at different areas around the pool. The trainers want to keep *the site the dolphin receives the reward* totally *unpredictable*.

In the dolphin's "mind," he should never know when the reward will come or where it will come from. If he is trained this way from the beginning, once the complete behavior is learned, disintegration of the whole behavior of swimming around the edges of the pool, does not occur. And as a bonus, he won't "jump" cues, either.

I made this mistake, too, as a young trainer, and the lesson has remained with me since. I neglected to pay attention to what the dolphin I was training was doing, and before I realized it, the dolphin was swimming in tiny circles and returning for a reward. Guess whose fault *that* was.

You and Your Dog

The same kinds of errors happen every day with owners attempting to train their dogs.

Let's say that, at the end of every day, you plan on taking ten minutes to train your dog. We will assume that your dog is trained to SIT, STAY, and COME.

Now, let's assume, too, that you train the dog *in the same sequence* every day. First, you tell the dog to SIT, then to STAY, and then to COME, and then you finally reward the dog. You repeat this sequence about six times during the session. Since dogs, like dolphins, are generally very intelligent animals, here's what is likely to happen:

Remember that you've determined that your dog likes his reward and will work for it. If he were a person, he would probably think, "When does he reward me?"

The the answer would be, "I'm rewarded every time for the *very last thing* that he asks me to do!"

In this case, that's *not* SITTING or STAYING. The third and last behavior he's performing is *coming to the trainer.*

If this scenario plays out on a consistent basis, you will begin to see the dog SIT and STAY for shorter and shorter periods. He is anxious to come to you, the trainer, to get his reward. You have now become predictable.

You've set up the same sequence of behaviors and the animal is responding to it. It is as if the behaviors have all merged into one.

The way to eliminate the problem is to become unpredictable. In other words, *change the sequence.*

For example, you might first have the dog SIT. Then, as the dog remains in that position, you might walk *to* the dog and reward him. Or you might tell the dog to COME from the very beginning, and reward him then.

As you can see, you've now changed things up, and you have become unpredictable. The dog is now forced to pay attention to *each command individually* to get a reward, and most importantly, YOU ARE NOW IN COMPLETE CONTROL of the dog's behavior.

In the world of animals, problems relating to predictability are *never* the fault of the animal—they come about because of a pattern of events usually initiated by the trainer. (Once in a while, unanticipated interruptions can play a part, like another person entering the room in the middle of training.)

It doesn't matter who or what you're training. If you're not aware of specifically *what* behaviors you are actually rewarding, you can easily fall into this trap.

Okay, So What Do I Do Now?

So you've made a mistake and your dog is doing something you didn't mean to reward. How does a trainer get rid of a problem like this when it begins to develop?

The first thing a trainer in this situation needs to do is take a look at himself and figure out what it is he is doing to make the situation predictable. Most experienced animal trainers will tell you that the first thing they'd do would be to randomly change the sequence of behaviors and do it periodically. (If you change the sequence of behaviors only once, after a while you'll find you have the same problem all over again.)

By making things a little more unpredictable, trainers eliminate an animal's tendency to start "jumping" cues. Training becomes more interesting, and hopefully fun, for the dog…because he'll never know which cue is coming up next.

Predictability and People

As a teacher or parent, you are in control. You dictate what will happen (and are responsible for what doesn't). You are in charge of what goes on throughout the day.

Because these are decisions that *you* are making, you may choose to do things in a set routine each day because of convenience. In some circumstances, this can be a good thing because generally knowing what to expect is important to employees and students, too. But there are times when doing things the same way every day might also have a negative impact.

Don't get me wrong here. There's nothing wrong with having a "set" schedule in the classroom, as long as that schedule is changed periodically. The reason you want to make that change every now and then is because, as you read earlier in the book, in moderate amounts, CHANGE IS REINFORCING. By simply changing the daily routine, you can create more variety and fun. Our interest and motivation to learn are enhanced when we're having fun.

The change itself is the reward.

CHAPTER 7
BODY LANGUAGE

The more time a trainer spends with an animal, the better his chances to understand and get to know that animal's particular body language. If the trainer has taken the time to develop a relationship with the animal, he's much more in tune to changes in the way, for instance, the animal may react to different sounds. He also is more aware of how the animal typically stands, looks at him, sits, floats, moves, turns around or is likely to express his excitement.

As an animal trainer, I can tell you firsthand that body language is always an indication of how comfortable or content an animal is in the situation.

The Trainer's Body Language

A trainer's body language impacts how the animal relates to him, too. Some animals may respond more positively to a trainer's movement than others. With these types of animals, simply standing in one place for an extended period of time can have a negative impact.

In other words, for those animals, if you are more animated, e.g., move around a bit more, the training session will be more interesting for the animal involved. It will help to sustain its motivation for learning.

Other times, the way a trainer stands can communicate a lack of self-confidence. New trainers especially tend to stand in a position directly facing the animal. Because it is completely "open" to the animal, it can make the trainer appear less relaxed, and, as a result, somewhat vulnerable. It depends on the type and personality of the animal.

Most animals need motivation and confidence to perform well, so it is rare that a trainer who stands in one place will have a positive impact on the animal. That's why, when you watch a good trainer in action, you'll see him tell a dog or sea lion to STAY, and then move around to different places in the room.

What this enhances more than anything is getting and keeping the animal's attention. If a trainer begins to move around from place to place, and does it on a free-moving and random basis, the animal's interest is sparked. Then, when the trainer randomly comes to the dog or sea lion and rewards him for staying, it not only makes performing the behavior reinforcing. It also keeps the animal interested in the training session.

The Body Language of Animals

The first step in interpreting an animal's body language is to note the way it either stands, sits, floats (with respect to dolphins, etc.) or lies "normally." There are a lot of things that may dictate this, like physical size and body shape, but it depends too on the natural personality of the individual animal.

For example, the normal body position of a high-strung dog is likely to be totally different from one that is more "mellow" because of their natural personalities. A dog that is high-strung is more likely to want to move around, whereas a more even-tempered animal is likely to remain in one place.

Eyes

Animals, like humans, express a lot through their eyes. Some dogs, for example, like being looked at directly in the eyes, while some see it as a threat. In my experience, the way an animal reacts when you look directly into his eyes is based on his relationship and trust in you.

Dogs, as you probably know, are animals that naturally run in packs. If a dog is unfamiliar with you, he may be confused as to where he fits into the "pack" in relationship to you. Because of this, when I visit an animal shelter, I try not to look directly into the eyes of dogs. It's likely that they are unsure of me and the environment as well.

My dog Foster likes having me look directly into his eyes, and he would be content to stare back at me all day long, but it wasn't always that way. When I adopted him, Foster was aggressive and stared at me, as in a challenge.

I avoided looking directly into his eyes because he took it as threatening. If I accidentally did, he would begin to growl, and become more aggressive. If I had tried to force the issue, his defensive behavior would have escalated.

So, in order to avoid giving that situation a chance to develop, I worked to extinguish his desire to stare at me in challenge. He never won a fight *because there was no fight.*

What changed? I don't know what happened to Foster before I met him, but over time, when he started to learn that I was his friend—one who had all these great things to offer him—he began to look at me for another reason. I had something he wanted. At the time of this writing, that was four years ago. He still stares at me, but his reason now is not because he is challenging me. Instead, he's seeking attention—he simply wants to be petted.

Dogs that are submissive or shy don't like being stared at directly either. Unlike more aggressive dogs, shy dogs tend to look away.

The moral of the story is this: Look into a new dog's eyes and pay close attention to his or her reaction. Use what you learn to guide your interactions with the dog until he becomes adjusted to you. If you are not aware, the situation may become progressively uncomfortable for the animal, and makes training much more difficult, if not impossible.

Movement

Does the dog like to naturally pace around or is he more sedentary? Knowing this helps you most when he *doesn't* do what he naturally does. If the dog is a pacer, for example, and you suddenly see him standing and staring at something, you will know to look for the reason his body language has changed. Likewise, if your dog normally is content to lie by your side, if he jumps up, he's reacting to something.

Knowing an animal's natural habits gives a trainer the opportunity to correct and even avoid problems, by acting to identify and correct, when necessary, catalysts for movements uncommon to it.

Marine Mammals

The body language of dolphins and whales is just as important as it is with dogs. A good trainer takes the time to know what is "normal" for a species of animal and what's "normal" for the individual animal he's working with.

As a rule, for instance, dolphins are fairly high-strung. They have a lot of energy and they get excited quite easily. If a dolphin is moving slowly, the first response of the trainer might be to assume that something is "wrong."

On the other hand, if a particular dolphin the trainer knows from experience with a particular dolphin that he's a slower and more sedentary animal, then the observation of that dolphin moving *quickly* might indicate that something had really excited it, that something truly unique had occurred. It all depends on what might be considered "normal" for the animal in question.

At first glance, you might think that killer whales exhibit minimal body language. The graceful movement of a killer whale is, admittedly, amazing.

However, as someone who has had the opportunity to train killer whales, I can assure you that when one wants to turn on a dime, he can take that four- to six-ton body of his and do it in an instant. The fun part is finding out why.

I've seen one sea lion jump off his seat and dive into the water followed by another right smack in the middle of a show. This is a very common occurrence during the spring and early summer as the male sea lions gain size and start establishing dominance.

The most amazing thing to me, though, was how often this seemed to happen just because of the way one animal looked at another.

Who really knows what goes on in their minds! But one thing's for sure—observing and responding to the body language of animals in training makes the process go much more smoothly.

People

By now you know where I'm going with this.

Observing the body language of people is equally important when you're in charge of teaching or managing people. Individuals do specific things and move in specific ways that give you clues you need to understand when something out of the ordinary happens. The only way, however, that you can be aware of changes in a person's manner is when you know what is and isn't typical behavior for that person. And that takes time.

As with dogs, eyes are a huge factor. The more you get to know someone, the more you know, just from their eyes, what makes a person comfortable or uncomfortable. When, after all, do you look away? When do you make eye contact? What are you trying to achieve?

While there is an endless list of characteristics to consider, people give us an equally endless set of clues to how they feel in given situations.

Let's imagine that you have a student whom you feel you know quite well. This student is rather quiet, slouches in his chair, walks fairly slowly, and doesn't socialize much with the other students. If you pay attention at all, you'd notice if one day he sat in his chair a little straighter, walked with a little more meaning toward the front of the class, and interacted more with the other students. If you are the supervisor or teacher, you might suspect that those dramatic changes are due to something you did or said. Which brings us back to *your* body language.

An essential part of identifying reasons for changes in an individual's body language is awareness of our own body language when we interact with him. Are your arms crossed or down by your sides? Did you offer your hand? Did you smile or frown?

For instance, we know that people very easily stop paying attention in a lecture-only situation when the teacher or speaker stands in one place for an extended amount of time. It happens for the same reason we see it happen in the training of dogs—the trainer becomes boring.

Take Tony Robbins, for example. One of the reasons he's so motivating and captivating is not only the content of his material, but also the way he talks, the way he moves, and the way he delivers the material.

What a good speaker does is really quite similar to what a good trainer does: The primary goal is to get and then keep the attention of those you're speaking to or training.

If I'm not paying attention, I'm not listening. And if I'm not listening, I'm not learning.

Focusing on our own body language and that of others is a first step to gaining and keeping the attention of those whose behavior we seek to influence, whether they're animals, students or employees.

And once again, it's taking the time to develop a trusting relationship that makes understanding another's body language possible.

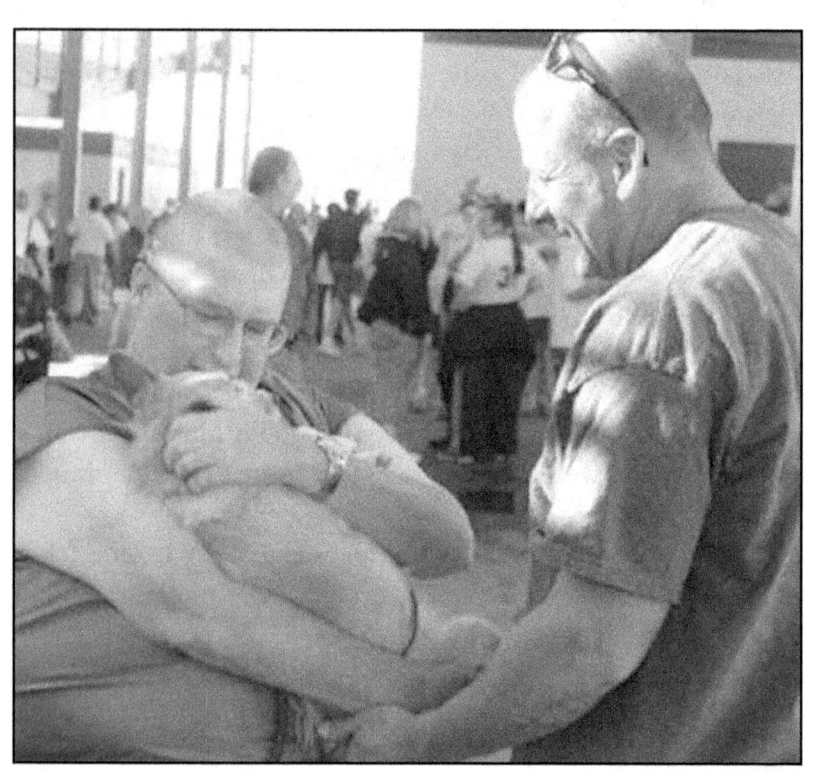

Chapter 8

MOTIVATION & ATTITUDE

Motivation has a huge impact on the training of any animal, and learning what motivates the animals I work with is one my favorite aspects of training.

The best animal trainers around are often very creative in finding the things that motivate the animals they are working with. But, in spite of that, the motivation and attitude of animals in training are quite often overlooked. Focusing just on training behaviors without considering what may "drive" an animal to complete those behaviors can be problematic.

When you're training an animal for a TV series or a commercial, "treats" will only go so far. After about the ninth or tenth "take," the treat reward alone will not "do the trick"; the animal has to be working for something more than just food or toys to guarantee a director four or five more successful takes.

The word motivation is used in a wide variety of settings to mean different things. Here's what I mean when I use the word. The reward which comes at the successful completion of a behavior—the "knowledge" of the animal that he will be rewarded—becomes the animal's *motivation* to perform the behavior correctly. The animal understands that when he performs a behavior, he will be rewarded (randomly) with something that he "likes," and that results in an increase in positive attitude and performance.

Motivation plays an important part in the training of just about any animal. After all, which animal do you think will be happier in a training session? The animal that has the motivation for knowing he will be rewarded for doing a behavior correctly, or one who is never rewarded, but rather is trained to do behaviors only because he's "forced" into it?

As we have also talked about before, what motivates one animal may not motivate another. Figuring out what the motivators are comes from getting to know an animal (developing a relationship), observing body language in response to various rewards and corrections, and laying the groundwork for trust.

Many things can dictate an animal's attitude and how motivated he is to learn, most of which are initiated and impacted by the trainer.

What some very successful animal trainers have found is that many times, an animal will "play" off of them. The animal's attitude will change according to what a trainer does or simply the way he acts. In other words, sometimes just doing something that's different can change an animal's attitude in a training session in a very positive way.

Dogs

I'll say it again. The motivators or rewards an astute trainer uses will normally vary from dog to dog. Finding out what most excites a given animal is a most valuable tool.

For instance, because golden retrievers normally like holding things in their mouths or playing with toys, a ball or another toy will usually motivate them. They may even like a variety of toys and balls. When on the set training a golden retriever for a scene in a commercial, I might begin by using a treat; then, after the seventh or eighth "take," as the dog begins to tire, I might switch to a ball or toy that he likes. This has prolonged many a filming session, helping to restore an animal's good attitude and motivation.

Other dogs have an incredible food drive. In these instances, the desire the animal has for food is a huge motivational factor which can be used quite successfully in training. When training a dog for whom food is a big motivator, the trainer who brings to the set a variety of foods to offer the animal can give himself the benefit of starting with one reward and then, after the seventh or eighth take, switching to different food reward. This will again increase the animal's motivation and attitude.

When all is said and done, though, the greatest thing about training dogs is this. Once the relationship between you and your dog has been established, the animal's motivation transfers from things like food and toys to something much more lasting. Now his primary motivation (and pleasure) come in pleasing you.

Marine Mammals

In training marine mammals, just as in dog training, time spent in developing a relationship with an animal lays a great foundation for sustaining motivation and attitude. When working with marine mammals, trainers leave them in the evening. Over time, the animals begin to look forward to seeing the trainers when they come to work each morning.

When I think of the days when I worked in theme parks, the most awesome thing I remember is coming in to work in the morning and seeing dolphins jumping out of the water in their excitement to see me. It certainly motivated me!

Building Attitude

As I watched my mentors and learned the philosophy behind their actions, I learned that sometimes it was not only important to reward an animal for doing the right thing, but equally as important to reward the animal's *attitude*.

I remember watching a very experienced trainer with a California sea lion, a very experienced five-year-old, 350-pound male who was a pro. The sea lion had been doing shows for about three years.

The training session was going on between shows, and it had gone a little longer than the trainer anticipated, but the sea lion was still hanging in there. He was seated at his podium and the trainer had been working with him to train him to use his flipper for a trick. (If you've ever seen a sea lion show, you know that the sea lion has a podium to rest his front flippers on.)

It was obvious that the animal became a little confused about what was expected of him. After a few minutes, I saw the trainer step back about 20 feet from the animal. He then waited about 10 seconds and called the sea lion to him. The sea lion jumped off his seat and slid over to the trainer on his belly the way sea lions do. The trainer rewarded the animal with about four pounds of fish.

I remember thinking to myself, "The trainer just had a problem with the animal. Why is he rewarding the animal for having such a hard time understanding what he wants?"

Then, as I continued to watch, the most amazing thing happened! The trainer sent the sea lion back to his seat, and from that point on, the animal's attitude changed and he began to do what the trainer wanted.

After the training session, I asked the trainer why he had done what he had. I still remember the answer as if it were yesterday. "I was rewarding his attitude."

He told me that he needed to do something to reward the animal because it wasn't the fault of the animal that he did not understand. Knowing that one of the easiest behaviors the sea lion could do was to jump off the podium and come to him, the trainer create an opportunity for the animal to experience "success," to be rewarded. Once accomplished, he brought the sea lion back to his seat and continued to train, hoping the animal's attitude would improve. And it did.

The animal's attitude immediately started to change, his motivation increased because he'd achieved some success, and the trainer made progress in training or correcting the behavior he was having problems with.

Through the years, I relived that incident over and over again in my mind, and I realized that what the trainer had to do to "reset" the situation was create a situation in which he could *legitimately reward the animal*. The sea lion's good "attitude" toward training was preserved by how the trainer rewarded his *persistence*, even in the face of repeated failure before.

Good or Bad, Attitudes are Contagious

Both good and bad attitudes really are contagious. We have all seen situations where there were good people running companies, and it seemed that everyone who worked for that company was a really thoughtful person. In my opinion, it all comes from the top.

I remember a company from a long time ago whose owners were simply not very nice people. They thought only about the "almighty dollar," were notorious for lying, treated everyone they worked with from other companies horribly, were impossible to work with, and were neither trusting nor to be trusted.

Over time, almost all the employees who stayed took on the exact same characteristics. They became just like the owners, in that they were also very negative, bitter, and unhappy people. The owners of that company spread their negativity and toxicity toward the entire group of employees.

Fortunately, I've also seen situations work the other way, too. From 1988 to 1992, I worked on the TV series "Empty Nest" on NBC, training the dog that appeared on the show.

When you have the luxury of working on a TV series with the right cast and crew, it can be a great experience, and that four-year period was one of the best times of my life.

Why was it that way? It all started with the management—the executive producers, associate producers, and producers. Simply put, they were all very nice people. So what type of people do you think they brought in to help with the show? People just like themselves. Intuitively, they developed authentic relationships and trust with their employees, made them feel important and needed, and made my working experience and that of everyone around them a great one!

It's easy to feel overwhelmed these days, like the sea lion in the story above. I wish more teachers, parents and managers would take the time to look deeply enough into what's going on around them to be able to see and reward true intentions.

If you're in a leadership position and someone is having problems learning or understanding what you are presenting or expecting of them, take time to accurately determine where the problem lies. Is the problem with me? Is that person really making the effort? At the very least, look for a way to acknowledge a good attitude before returning to the task at hand, just as my training mentor did.

Chapter 9

PRACTICE MAKES PERFECT

I've been a professional animal trainer for over 30 years, and in that time, I've made more than my share of mistakes. So will you. The key to making the training experience enjoyable for both you and the animals and people you train (as with just about anything else worth doing) is learning the principles and techniques developed by those who've gone before you and applying them in your own situation.

For those of you who, before reading this book, had never heard of any of the concepts involved in animal training (and even for those who had), I want to leave you with a final review of the basic concepts we've talked about here. If you remember these principles, I guarantee that you will be rewarded by the improvement you see in the behavior of your pets, your kids, your students, your employees, *and* yourself.

BOND WITH YOUR HEART...

One more time. The difference between a good trainer and a great trainer is...

Great trainers bond with their animals first. They learn what their pets like (and don't like), what rewards them and what doesn't, what scares them and what excites them... in short, they get to know them, developing a relationship based on trust. It's the foundation without which training can become rote and uninteresting. In a word, boring.

In the end, with most animals, food isn't the greatest reward. It's respect, interest, affection, trust. It's knowing you're important, appreciated, that you've made someone proud. It's the relationship. Develop the relationship first and you'll never be sorry.

...TRAIN WITH YOUR BRAIN

Operant Conditioning

All of the techniques used in animal training are based on research begun by B.F. Skinner. In its simplest form, the idea is this: Learned behaviors are motivated or de-motivated by what happens as a result of our doing them. If the result is "good" for us (reinforcement) we do whatever we did again. If it isn't (punishment), we don't.

- **Reinforcement** is *"an event, a circumstance, or a condition that increases the likelihood that a given response will recur."*
- **Punishment** is the *"presentation of an adverse event or outcome that causes a decrease in the behavior it follows."*
  - **Positive** *punishment involves the presentation of an unfavorable event or outcome in order to weaken the response it follows.*
  - **Negative** *punishment occurs when a favorable event or outcome is removed after a behavior occurs.*

Reinforcing behaviors is generally accomplished with rewards, namely the giving of something experienced as positive when a desired behavior occurs, like a food treat to a dog, or a trip to a favorite restaurant for a child who brings home a good report card.

Punishment is intended as a correction, and can come in two forms: 1) providing something experienced as negative when an undesired behavior occurs, or 2) taking away something experienced as positive when an undesired behavior occurs.

Being sent to time out for hitting your brother falls in the first category; *not* rewarding a dolphin when it fails to jump to the desired height falls in the other.

Get these concepts firmly in your mind, as everything else builds on this foundation.

Rewards

Different animals respond to different rewards. So it is with people, too. If you've done a good job in developing a relationship with your trainee, you'll know what kinds of things reinforce him or her, and be able to use them to communicate that they've done a good job.

But remember to change things up. Variation in the reward and the timing of its delivery can be even more reinforcing, and it helps to reduce the likelihood that an animal will "jump" cues, offering the desired behavior even before you've asked for it.

With children and animals especially, vary the order in which you do things, and surprise them. Be creative and unpredictable with rewards and you'll keep things interesting and fun.

Correction vs. Punishment

Some of my peers in the animal training industry are against the use of punishment, but I think that's because they misunderstand the context of the word. In this case, as mentioned in the section on operant conditioning, punishment isn't beating a dog or causing anyone real pain, as some might think. That's why I call what I do "correcting."

Think about it. There is no easy way to eliminate "bad" behavior habits, whether we're talking about dogs jumping up on guests or me messing up typing O's and I's, without first stopping the undesired habit. Remember, the mere completion of a behavior, even a bad one, is reinforcing.

Once you've taken away the "reward" for completing a bad behavior by *not allowing it to happen*, you go back to the drawing board over and over until the desired behavior is performed and you can reinforce it with a true reward.

Break Complex Behaviors into Incremental Steps

Where birds and other "small-brained" animals may be content (and maxed out) with learning and performing simple behaviors over and over, dogs and marine mammals and people aren't. Remember that most of the behaviors we learn to perform, even as infants, are more complex by nature than we tend to think. Learning to walk doesn't happen in one step, now does it?

So, whether you're teaching piano to a child or training your dog to roll over, the process involves more than a single behavior. It involves a sequence of incremental steps. First, the child learns the notes on two-dimensional sheets, then she learns which notes correspond to which keys, then to put her fingers on certain keys...

But, no matter how many steps there are, the rules of the game don't change. They're all still about rewards and corrections...and moving through the sequence; then by completing the entire behavior, you are actually reinforcing it.

Then, as each successive behavior is learned, reinforce it with appropriate rewards and corrections (if needed): the "bar" is raised, just as it is with dolphins we train to bow, and students who reach higher achieve even more.

Use Predictability Wisely

Predictability is important in the early going. Just as "one swallow doesn't make a summer," neither does giving a reward once for a behavior guarantee repetition. The learning is in the association of behavior and reinforcement, which only comes when it happens often enough to establish a pattern.

Once learned, however, sustaining the quality of performance depends on *unpredictability*. Being intermittently rewarded refreshes the connection between the behavior and "feeling good" and makes it more likely to be repeated.

Unpredictability is bad news when we talk about correction, however, not only in its consistency, but in its result. Use the same correction for the same "bad" behavior every time, or you risk the trainee's being rewarded simply because the behavior is completed.

Observe Body Language - Yours and Theirs

We receive clues from others about how they are feeling every day—arms crossed vs. open, smiles vs. frowns, standing face to face or turned to the side...

Body language is important enough that some trial lawyers use body language consultants to help them select juries in sensitive cases.

Animals take cues based on body language, too. If frightened or aggressive, having a human lock gazes with them can increase their fear or tendency toward aggression.

Stay loose and animated during any training session, and you communicate that you're open, interested, and not afraid yourself.

Motivation and Attitude—It's About You

The last, and perhaps most important, thing I want you to take away from this book is that your own attitude is contagious. You as a leader of animals or people dictate their moods and motivations in training situations just by the way you act.

As I said at points throughout this small guide, when in a training situation, you experience a problem, the first place to look is at yourself.

Do you inspire loyalty? Do your children, students, employees trust you? If so, expect them to work hard to gain your approval. If not, figure out what you may be doing (or not doing) to facilitate the training process.

Are you having no impact when trying to change a negative behavior? Pay attention and look for ways *you* may be reinforcing the behavior accidentally.

Did you go straight into training and not spending enough time developing a relationship with the animal or person you were working with? Do you draw a blank when asked what most motivates the students in your class or the group you supervise? If so, it's okay: the first step is to correct your own misbehavior. Stop where you are and get to know them personally. You don't have to spend time with them socially, but you do need to know each of them well enough to predict what rewards work for each and what do not.

One More Time

The key to successful animal and people training is in learning what rewards and corrections work best with the individual you are raising, teaching, coaching or managing, then being unpredictable with rewards and consistent with corrections, breaking complex behaviors down into smaller steps where success can be experienced and rewarded, and making the learning or work environment emotionally safe and comfortable.

There's only one way I know to do that: by taking the time to establish and maintain a trusting relationship and then using scientifically-proven methods that have been in use in animal training for almost 100 years.

Bond with your heart. Train with your brain.

A Few Last Cues

As a professional animal trainer, I've had the opportunity to enjoy a career that involves the training of dogs, sea lions, dolphins, killer whales, and a variety of other intelligent animals. What I learned about all the animals I've met in the three decades I've been involved, has helped me to understand people, too. We both feel love and pain, we both need companionship and friendship, we both feel safe when we are understood.

Because I trained marine mammals early in my career, the training techniques I developed for use with dogs were heavily influenced by my experiences there. Effective parenting, education and management develops over time from a variety of experiences, as well.

I had a host of very good teachers at the time, so I began to listen and learn. I began to understand and work with the techniques of one's style of training, but over time I added ideas from another, and eventually began to add ideas of my own. In the end, I came up with my own style of training, and that has been the most fun.

The same thing applies to good parenting, management, or teaching. A person may learn to do things a certain way, establish a basic idea, and then branch off, using his or her own unique methods and style.

But the *best* animal trainers I've ever seen never change, in that they're humble and empathetic, and good students themselves. They never stop learning, even when they are in charge. *Especially* when they're in charge.

You can be one of them. Here's to good training!

About Joel Silverman

Joel Silverman turned a childhood dream into a lifelong career of training and performing with the animals he loved so much. From his early days in the 70's and 80's, Joel found himself working in nearly every theme park in Southern California. Whether he was training killer whales at Sea World, dolphins at Knott's Berry Farm and Magic Mountain, or birds, dogs, and cats at Universal Studios, Joel adapted the techniques he developed in the 70's and 80's to launch a successful career in training animals to star in live shows, Hollywood films, television programs and commercials.

In 2014, Joel starred in a commercial as part of Chase Bank's national campaign where he had six dogs rolling over at the same time. His dog Duchess was also featured grabbing the receipt at the end of the commercial.

As host of the popular television series "Good Dog U" on cable's "Animal Planet," Joel had the opportunity to showcase his unique ability to help owners train their dogs and deal with problem behaviors. From 2011-2014 he hosted his nationally syndicated TV series "What Color is Your Dog?" His own blend of training comes from a combination of dog training techniques as well as those used with dolphins, sea lions, and killer whales.

Joel has appeared on hundreds of national and local morning TV shows, as well as radio news programs. Joel has offered advice on pet care and training based on his lifetime commitment to the welfare of animals and their special place in our lives. His efforts on behalf of animal rescue and welfare organizations are well known. They are Joel's personal and professional priority.

In 1986, Joel received The Behavior of the Year Award from I.M.A.T.A. (International Marine Animal Trainers Association), and the 2008 Dog Trainer of the Year Award at the 54th Annual Show Dogs of the Year Awards at the Westminster Dog Show.

Joel Silverman's Dog Trainer Certification Courses

In January, 2017 Joel launched his Joel Silverman's Dog Trainer Certification Courses. These courses JSDT1, JSDTF, and JSDT2, are for people wanting to become certified dog trainers. During these unique four and five-day hands-on programs, Joel travels across the United States and uses humane societies as his home base. There, the students use untrained dogs Joel has picked out to teach for his courses. Every student has their hands on every dog at every phase of each behavior that is taught. Of course the takeaway, is that these dogs have a better chance of being adopted. This is great for owners of dog day-care businesses looking to add dog training, people wanting to become dog trainers, professional dog trainers, and volunteers and employees at humane societies and animal shelters. If you are interested in becoming a dog trainer, or are a humane society looking to take part, please check out our website at www.joelsilverman.net.

Other Books By Doce Blant Publishing

More What Color Is Your Dog

Paperback
ISBN 978-0-9965702-9-9

Hardbound
ISBN 978-0-9967622-0-5

eBook
ISBN 978-0-9967622-1-2

www.doceblantpublishing.com

www.ingramcontent.com/pod-product-compliance
Lightning Source LLC
Chambersburg PA
CBHW052057070526
44584CB00017B/2215